LISTENING

AS A WAY

OF

BECOMING

LISTENING
AS A WAY
OF
BECOMING

Earl Koile

Regency Books

a division of
Word Books, Publisher
Waco, Texas

Quotation at beginning of chapter 4 is from "Mending Wall"
from *The Poetry of Robert Frost* edited by Edward Connery
Lathem. Copyright 1930, 1939, © 1969 by Holt, Rinehart and
Winston. Copyright © 1958 by Robert Frost. Copyright © 1967
by Lesley Frost Ballantine. Reprinted by permission of Holt,
Rinehart and Winston, Publishers.

ISBN 0-87680-510-1
Library of Congress catalog card number: 76-48520
Printed in the United States of America

For Carmon and our children—
Kimberle, Kristen, and Stephen

Contents

Foreword

For more than three decades I have been observing expressions of a major change, or pattern of changes, in our society. As industrialization advances people are more and more constrained to locate themselves, group themselves, even define themselves in accord with the demands of production. The resulting social mobility, age-grading and accent on individual success have eroded the ties of family, friendship, and community so that loneliness and anomie have become pervasive. Television helps us all to take this situation for granted. Rarely are we permitted to see on television anything faintly resembling a normal relationship between two people. For that matter, we are rarely permitted to see any real people; instead we are offered a monotonous parade of clowns and psychopaths.

A consequence of the fragmentation of society, the alienation of people one from another, and the dehumanizing influences upon us all has been the springing up of a thriving "loneliness business." There are singles bars, computer dating services, various kinds of encounter groups, gurus, all promising relationship and community but often leaving people more lonely than before.

Psychologists, it must be said, have had a part in all this. Distorting or oversimplifying certain aspects of established theory, they have helped to spread the idea that it is through "openly expressing emotion," "getting in touch with feelings," "releasing locked up potential," that one will find friendship and success. The big trouble is that too often, amid all this focusing on the self and its expression, no attention is given to the wishes of others. The result is that the only relationship attained is one between the self and an object, and the community so eagerly sought is either illusory or transitory. In short, while many are "expressing" nobody is listening.

Now comes Earl Koile with his welcome message of good sense and good will: it is not through expressing ourselves but through listening to others that we increase our self-awareness and, at the same time, begin developing new relationships or reconstructing old ones.

I have taken particular satisfaction from this book because it gives strong evidence that my colleagues and I have been on the right track. In interviewing people from various walks of life, we have had the strong impression that people today rarely have a chance to talk about their deeper concerns. Accordingly, when a situation is structured so that listening is the order of the day people almost always pour out their hearts, telling us with enthusiasm of the benefits they received from being interviewed. But the great beauty of interviewing is that it works the other way 'round as well. It improves the interviewer as well as the interviewee. Dr. Koile makes abundantly clear why this should be so.

Earl Koile's book makes us want to listen. He is too tactful to say so but he knows very well that all of us most of the time, and some of us all the time, had rather put in our two cents worth than hear what others have to say. We need exemplars of good listening, and we need knowledge of how to go about doing what we know we should. On both counts Dr. Koile serves us well. In his courageous and warm-hearted book he makes most of his points by telling us of his own experience of becoming a listener and of becoming through listening. At the same time he makes it clear that listening is a form of social behavior that can be studied objectively.

We can conceptualize the various social and psychological processes that influence listening, we can define and measure variables, and we can construct research designs. It is not unlikely that a new area of conventional social psychological research is here being opened up. One may hope, however, that whoever carries out this kind of inquiry will first apprehend the richness, the complexity, and the knowledge of acquaintance that can come only through the kind of personal account that we are offered here. What is most fortunate is that one can study listening only by listening, or by persuading others to do so. This means that those who are involved in research on listening will benefit from its processes as well as from its results.

NEVITT SANFORD
President, The Wright Institute

Berkeley, California
1977

Preface
and Acknowledgments

What does it mean for you to listen to me and for me to listen to you? So very much! It means that we are more apt to listen to ourselves with more care and understanding. It means that having heard ourselves we may be able to pay more attention to other people and things that matter all around us. My listening to you becomes a reminder that there are people in the world besides me. It is more. It is a way I come to know myself. It is a way I come to know you.

Our fear, our hurt, and our loneliness often separate us. So does our joy. This is especially true when we lose our ability to tune into ourselves and to one another through listening. Listening is a way of touching and being touched. Once we lose our listening touch, we may no longer feel compassion for those in pain. We may no longer share their joy. If I lose my sensitivity for you, I risk losing my sensitivity to other people and to other forms of life—to a flower, to a bird—and to nature's creations.

To talk about listening only in abstract terms is to remove ourselves from the experience of listening. I have, therefore, presented in this book anecdotes to illustrate listening experiences—mine and others. I have attempted to talk about listening so that you can become your own listener—with me, with the people presented, with yourself alone, or perhaps with people you bring along from your own experiences as you read. My hope is that you will become a part of the listening experiences shared here in ways that fit for you.

While writing this book I felt deep gratitude for Carl Rogers, one of my teachers with whom I have had many learning experiences—although never a class—and whose life and work have enriched me. Throughout my professional life I have been greatly influenced by him—as a person, a therapist, and as a writer who has fired my imagination. It is he who, without knowing it, has sustained me during hours when I could not listen to anyone, including myself. I can lay no claim to being Rogerian. There is only one, and that is Carl Rogers himself. And he probably has more freedom and flexibility in changing what it means to be Rogerian than anyone who might lay claim to that way of being, to that orientation, or to that point of view toward psychology.

I want to express the special gratitude and appreciation I feel for several persons who were involved in the preparation of this book. My wife, Carmon, read and reread early drafts and the final manuscript, giving always a critical eye and special care. Keith Miller paid me the tribute and gave me the gift of being as critical with my work as he is with his own, and he spurred gently when I faltered. Marjorie Menefee read critically as an editor and as a clinician to help me stay out of the jargon and yet stay in whatever substance is here. Dina Edens scrutinized the manuscript as person-woman-wife-mother-social worker, and, among other useful suggestions, insisted that long sentences be turned into shorter ones.

Patricia Woods Prewitt often had more faith in me than I had in myself when she saw promise in early drafts that I wanted to throw away. Cathy Leary, Tom DiNardo, and Steve Haunschild shared ideas and anecdotes generously from their own experiences; their animated and enthusiastic attitudes were nicely contagious. Bert Kruger Smith read an early draft and reviewed with care and detail ways to achieve focus and organization of the material. Sue Wade read and played back, with her usual intellectual acuteness, varied interpretations and inferences that might be drawn from some of the incidents and anecdotes.

Shirley Bird Perry, with whom I have conducted many human relations workshops, tenaciously insisted that some of the experiences be shared in writing. Joyce Frost and Jack Dunham read parts of the manuscript and offered perspectives from their fields of speech and the psychology of learning, respectively. Gaby Rappaport offered the perspectives of a university senior with refreshing interests in learning whatever and whenever she could.

My former students, persons with whom I have been associated in workshops, training seminars, and in individual and group therapy, along with some of my colleagues at the University of Texas at Austin, have been, in effect, collaborators in the experiences on which this book is based. I owe much to the Department of Educational Psychology where value is placed not only on theory and research in different areas of psychology, but on the application of knowledge. It is a department where faculty members are encouraged to take the time to write and to reach audiences beyond the campus in their areas of interest and expertise.

The anecdotes and incidents throughout this book are based on actual experiences. Material quoted is based on recordings, written reactions from the persons involved, and on notes reconstructed following a particular experience. In some instances the material has been condensed. Naturally, the names of persons have been changed to provide privacy.

EARL KOILE

Austin, Texas

1. Someone to Listen

Not to have known . . . either the
mountain or the desert is not to have
known one's self. Not to have known
one's self is to have known no one.

Joseph Wood Krutch

At a faculty meeting the other day, while listening to a colleague with whom I had felt wary and distant, I became aware of feelings of warmth toward him—liking, almost. I was puzzled, until I began to sense that his bluster and assertiveness were only an outer coating—peanut brittle hiding a marshmallow center of constant compassion. Strange that I had listened to him so many times and had not heard this softer side. Or had I really bothered to listen before? I know that often I fail to hear many of my own inner messages and then, suddenly, for no clear reason, I tune in deeply and hear something new.

This commonplace incident reminded me of how insensitive and blind I can be to alternative ways of looking at other people and at myself. It also reminded me of how much I try to avoid changes in my life, even some that I claim to be seeking. Often I resolve to take more time for leisure and spend less time working only to find myself using the "leisure time" working. I am just as likely to discover that I have stopped work in the middle of a project and am being leisurely, enjoying it immensely. And the leisure was not even "on my schedule"! What such an experience tells me is that my work is sometimes my leisure and that my resolve to change my schedule may not actually suit my needs. I am out of touch with my inner desires. Similarly, when I maintain a stereotypic view of another person, I am out of touch with what that person is like, just as I was with my colleague until I listened to him anew.

I have trouble remembering the rewards of being more attuned, of listening with more sharpness to myself and to people around me. Often I become so occupied with daily routines I am unable to tune into my own desires to try to discover and rediscover the roots of what I want to do and be in my life—today, tomorrow, next week.

LISTENING AS SELF-RENEWAL

A recurring problem for me is that my feelings of self-worth too often are based on what I do, what I produce in some tangible way. As a consequence, my attention focuses on familiar symbols of success—activities to be recognized, credentials to be acclaimed, objects to be collected. The results of my striving, I hasten to add, are not entirely bad. But the more obvious symbols of achievement in themselves have not brought me the deepest joy and the most abiding sense of self-worth. My greatest and most enduring feelings of value have come through caring deeply for others and in experiencing their caring for me. Such caring comes through listening, I feel like a terribly slow learner in acknowledging that only in recent years have I come to learn that *listening* is a primary way by which I can become a significant person in my own eyes and in the eyes of others. And I must continually relearn it.

It is no accident, then, that I am immersed in a listening profession. I can combine my need to "do something" with my desire to "be someone" in relationships with other people. In the seminaries there is a well-known saying that one way to keep your religion is to become a minister. This statement certainly applies to me in my work. My involvement in a mental health profession has obvious payoffs for me, especially as I am enhanced through listening to others and being heard by them.

Listening to ourselves and others is a way of becoming more as persons. It is a part of our search for ourselves. It is the ancient quest for self-knowledge about which wise men, poets, and scholars have written through the ages. Seeking self-knowledge requires listening to ourselves and involves a personal language of self-revelation. Using that language, we embark on personal journeys inward to discover what is there, perhaps to rediscover that which we already know, and to confront our human problems— sometimes resolving them, sometimes not. If we are fortunate, we may discover ways of living without daily formulas. If there is a formula, it may have to do with discovering life as it is lived and finding that it is predictable and unpredictable; enhancing and self-defeating; joyful and hurtful; and, for most of us, full of promise for being truly worth living.

Our sense of identity and part of our nature as human beings hinge on our ways of talking and listening to ourselves. We distinguish ourselves one from another and

21

from other parts of nature through our ways of feeling and of sharing who we are. Our inner dialogues influence how we respond to art, music, and to the inspiration we find in nature and spiritual life. Our sense of aliveness comes from an inner attitude of hope and belief in our own worth.

Our ways of hearing, then, are parts of the personality that are uniquely our own. Ways we listen influence our capacity for both cooperation and independence in relationships without blind conformity to the norms and pressures of any particular group. We can relate to others —individually, in groups, in organizations—and enhance them and ourselves, perhaps even transcend ourselves. What is important is that we not lose our separateness or give up responsibility for decisions as individuals. The more we unthinkingly turn ourselves over to a group or to a social enterprise, the greater the loss and detachment we suffer within. John Gardner has appropriately called it "inner estrangement and outer conformity."[1] Listening to one another and sharing our lives become means by which we nourish a sense of community in relationships and nourish also our freedom and individuality.

Through listening, we help each other to search and find what in our lives is of value, and what seems to hold value beyond us in the lives of other people. When I no longer search or care about what matters in my life and in yours, I have lost faith and have stepped over its boundary into hopelessness.

In sorting out values and charting directions, my goal need not be to find the right answers for all time. To seek

---

[1] John W. Gardner, *Self Renewal* (New York: Harper & Row, 1963), p. 94.

only answers is to ignore the possibility that a commitment to the search *itself* may be a life-giving part of
whatever answer there is. Listening deeply to myself and
to others is a part of this life-giving search and commitment. Who will listen to me? This may be my cry in time
of need! But, To whom can I listen? may be the question
and the commitment that sustain me.

WHO WILL LISTEN?

With whom can you share some of your deepest concerns, your lows, your highs, your doubts, your convic-
tions? Who will listen? Who shares with you? And will
you listen? It is not always easy to be good listeners or to
have others who will listen to us. Caring and trustworthy
give-and-take relationships in which we have little need
to put one another up or down, or to insist on change, are
hard to come by. Friends may be few. Most relationships
may be casual. Even some that offer intimacy and promise
depth and permanence may turn out to be transient.

We cannot always rely on friends and members of our
family to listen and understand. Families and friends see
and hear us so often and in so many ways that their eyes
lose their sharpness and their ears may miss our meaning. We may get locked into restricted ways of sharing
and hearing among people with whom we live and work.
They may see us with a gaze too fixed and hear us with
an ear too constant. People close to us often have trouble
separating themselves from us. They may project too
much of their meaning into what they hear. Our continuous contacts and awareness of one another eventually can
lead to no awareness at all.

Could strangers listen more perceptively and understand us better than family or friends? How much dare we share or ask of strangers? A stranger's knowledge of us is limited. People who have little stake in our lives also may have little stake in listening or caring. Yet, under some conditions, they may be useful in mirroring different facets of our behavior. They may listen and have the keen awareness of someone who sees us afresh.

If friends, associates, and our family become too involved with us to see and hear us in sharp perspective, and if strangers lack involvement and know us too little, to whom do we turn? Out of such a dilemma—the need to be heard and understood, the lack of someone to turn to—literally millions of people have entered individual and group psychotherapy, religious study groups, and interpersonal relations groups of one kind or another. Millions more watch television. Many among all these, and still others, remain lonely and unheard.

This is an age of mass communication in which we can be reached with a flick of our television switches, but we cannot reach back. We have not yet attained a contemporary era of personal communication in which we share and listen in depth to reach one another. Still, the language of sharing and listening, experienced in personal terms, offers relief from boredom, loneliness, and anxiety. But only when our feelings are heard and understood are we likely to be enabled to form deeper personal relationships and to break unsatisfactory personal behavior patterns. Clues for a happier, more effective life may be found when we can listen sensitively and openly to others and they to us. Moreover, in such interchanges we may find healthy outlets for our anger and frustration, richer ways to experience love and joy, and, in short, find new dimensions of our humanness. The use of a personal language of listening and sharing in dealing with our

24

human problems and cultivating our humanness is central in the pages that follow.

PICTURES OF WHAT WE HEAR

For me, listening in personal terms to someone becomes visual. I usually see pictures as I hear words. The words portray vivid images, and both yield meaning. Through the years famous raconteurs have fascinated and moved us to the edges of our chairs with picturesque details and action-packed drama. Listening to what we see, not simply to the words we hear, adds a new dimension, along with richness in depth and detail. We become more identified, involved.

The Collage

You can see Melanie's picture of herself as a child when she says, "I am standing on a street corner—dirty, poor, in a ragged dress much too large, and barefooted. I am filled with sadness and shame. I feel forsaken and forlorn." Even now her face as she sits a few feet away resembles that of an unwanted, neglected child. She slumps in the chair; her head is down; and tears stream down her face.

In a tone of firmness, Melanie continues, "I hide my dirty little kid image. I barely ever let myself think about her. But when she comes up and into view, I feel terribly angry with her and want to punish her." Then, more softly, "But I also want to hold her and care for her and protect her from grown-ups."

Looking at Melanie, I can see that she is an attractive young woman in her late twenties, impeccably groomed and wearing a designer dress. Still, she shows the little

girl side of herself that feels fearful, rejected, and un-
lovable.

I need to remember that Melanie's pictures are shaped,
textured, and tinted with a mixture of discordant emotions. If I see her self-portrayal literally, I will miss the
meaning. At a counseling session a few weeks back, I saw
a different but related childhood picture. "I grew up in a
twenty-two-room house with many servants," she had
said. "It was a quiet, lonesome place, and I came home
mostly for vacations from boarding school, which I attended from the age of five through high school."

The literal pictures of the poor, dirty waif on the street
and of the rich little girl in the big house do not fit. The
emotional portraits of loneliness, self-pity, and rejection
fit rather well. Melanie lives in a big house now, and, as
she describes it and her loneliness in it, the pictures of
her past and present form a collage for the mind's eye.

In the foreground of the collage is a woman. Behind
her is the image of a "dirty little kid" of whom the
woman disapproves. Off to the side the woman hides the
girl—the bad, sad, hurt, and angry parts of herself. Now
she brings the child out of hiding, protecting and comforting her in her feelings of rejection, loneliness, and dependence. The woman and the child struggle over staying
separate and becoming one. The collage of Melanie por-
trays many scenes of conflict. My hope is that she will
allow herself to see and feel the relatedness of the
scenes, and eventually feel less fragmented and more
whole.

The Dancers

In the therapy group we were talking about the restric-
tions that we felt in touching other people. We heard

26

Sally say, "I grew up in a family of girls. Our parents approved of our dancing together at home." We could see her dancing and laugh with her when she added, "But we had to dance with pillows between us. We were never allowed to touch stomachs or other parts of our bodies, except our arms and hands, when we danced." Sally grew up learning that touching meant sex. "And now," she said more seriously, "I am beginning to learn that touching does not need to be sexual, that it can mean I care; I feel gentle; I touch you as a gift, freely given."

Substituting My Own Pictures

The vivid pictures we get as we listen to others may not always help. Recollections of our own past may distract us, or the imagery may become so real that we react unpredictably and inappropriately. Many years ago I was conducting a training workshop for counselors and other mental health workers. As a part of the workshop we used practice interviews to experience how we used ourselves in one-to-one relationships. We wanted also to examine how we listened and responded to people as they shared their problems.

The workshop setting was a large comfortable room with a small platform in the center that we used for demonstration interviews—something like a theater in the round. I was interviewing a young man of nineteen, a college sophomore who had volunteered to share some things that were bothering him. He had recently moved to campus from his family's farm. He expressed resentment toward his father who, in his eyes, was a taskmaster around the farm. He said that he could seldom please his father and was tired of trying. Still, he needed his father's support, financially and emotionally.

27

He began to share an incident to illustrate his dilemma. His father had insisted that he replace some damaged shingles on the lower roof of the cowbarn. The hitch was that he had to do it on a Saturday afternoon when he had planned to go to town with his friends. Showing disgust, he said, "And to make it worse, after being so mad for having to change my plans and work, I lost my footing and slipped off the roof. And I landed on top of a great big pig."

In that instant the ludicrous scene this young man had painted was so vivid for me I had to laugh. I began with a smile and a chuckle, then erupted into unrestrained, almost hysterical laughter. To make the situation worse, my mind's eye immediately recalled boyhood scenes of pig races, scenes in which my two cousins and I would try to ride and race the larger hogs on my grandfather's farm. And my laughter continued. Finally, I looked up, hoping that the young man had joined me in appreciating the humor of the situation. He was not laughing. His face was sober. Actually, he was looking at me in astonishment.

I regained composure and apologized, briefly sharing the recollection of my own pig riding. He looked straight at me, not at all forgiving, and added, "But if the pig hadn't been there, I might have hurt myself." This most sensible observation also struck me as funny. This time, however, I was able to maintain my composure. I sat quietly for a few seconds to shake loose my emotional state and get back in touch with this young man in a more serious vein.

Finally, I could listen to him again and he could express his concerns with increasing freedom. My listening, however, had been tested, and, for a few minutes, found sorely lacking. I also had the workshop participants to face. About half of them reacted as I did, but the others

were quite vexed that I could be so insensitive and out
of control. I expressed regret for the laughter, but at the
same time I acknowledged that I enjoyed it.

When we get caught, whether in tears or laughter, in
the scenes we see as we listen, the consequences may not
seem so off-base if our reactions match those of the person to whom we are listening. When our reactions do not
match, however, we probably have left their scene and
created our own. That is what happened to me.

WE STAND IN NEED

The chapters that follow are interlaced with incidents
from my own life and the lives of a countless number of
people. These experiences show the versatility in ways
we listen, the impact of actually being heard, and the
often unexamined ties between many facets of our personality and our listening patterns. Many of the anecdotes
demonstrate emotional traps in which we may find ourselves. Others describe patterns of behavior that may serve
us well. Emphasis is on the dynamics, the connectedness,
and the flow of behavior but much is said also about
resolution of conflicts, approaches to solutions to problems, and living with ambiguity.

The people whose experiences are shared represent
many occupations and professions. Several undergradu-
ates and graduate students in diverse areas of specializa-
tion are included as well. My association with these
people ranges from a few hours to many years. They and
I at one time or another have experienced burdensome
emotional turmoil. Most of us have discovered that we
are not alone in what we experience and what we feel
but at one time or another have felt alone and have
known the piercing pain of that aloneness.

Some of us have sought out different forms of counseling and psychotherapy—individual and group. We may have bootlegged a little therapy on the side. Bootlegged therapy is personal therapeutic help that we get in the guise of something else—classes, seminars, professional training workshops, study groups of one kind or another, and personal show-and-tell sessions with friends and colleagues. Bootlegged therapy often can be helpful. It allows us plenty of room to seek personal help, to tell our story and be heard, in congenial settings with supportive relationships. But it can be hazardous. We may use it to minimize or deny to ourselves our need for guided personal help from a trained professional.

Are the people seen in therapy representative in any way of people in the general population? In his book *Man's Search for Himself*, Rollo May says, "By and large they are the ones for whom the conventional pretenses and defenses of the society no longer work. Very often they are the more sensitive and gifted members of the society; they need to get help, broadly speaking, because they are less successful at rationalizing than the 'well-adjusted' citizen who is able for the time being to cover up his underlying conflicts."[2] Dr. May then suggests that the people who seek therapeutic assistance "provide a very revealing and significant barometer of the conflicts and tensions under the psychological surface of the society. This barometer should be taken seriously, for it is one of the best indexes of the disruptions and problems which have not yet, but may soon, break out widely in the society."[3]

Many of the people whom I have come to know, regard-

---

[2] Rollo May, *Man's Search for Himself* (New York: Signet Books, 1967), p. 16.
[3] Ibid., p. 17.

less of their association with therapy in any form, hunger for ideas, relationships, and a host of experiences that will enliven them and bring purpose and vibrancy to their lives. One of the biggest problems in satisfying this hunger is getting beyond the veneers with which we try to tell each other that all is well in our worlds. We hold back from other people, sometimes with good reason.

It is trite to say, as the poets have said eloquently and often, that we forever stand in need of one another. Yet we do. In order to get a feel for who I am, and, later, for who you are, I need your help. But I do *not* need for you to define me. Rather, I need you as a listening post with whom I can compare, confirm, or revise my own self-definitions. It is audacious, even foolish, for either of us to define the other. But surely there are gains for us if we can accompany one another in discovering more about ourselves—as separate people and as people together. Moments of discovery might bring twinges of pain or twists of perspective that surprise. But they also might be sprigged with touches of beauty and joy. And if we could let ourselves, in full consciousness, listen to and feel the meanings and the struggles of each other, we "would be flying with the eagle and growing with the grass." [4]

――――――
[4] *Baja California and the Geography of Hope,* ed. Kenneth Brower; photographs by Eliot Porter, text by Joseph Wood Krutch (San Francisco: Sierra Club, 1967), p. 66.

2. Hearing Compliments and Criticism

*The greatest compliment that was ever paid
me was when one asked me what I thought,
and attended my answer.*

Henry David Thoreau

During an early session of a therapy group, members were sharing some of their impressions of each other. Margaret, an attorney in her late thirties, was saying, "Despite your efforts to come on hard-nosed, I see you as a most sensitive and loving person, a little shy, but also impish, and as having a marvelous sense of humor." I glanced up and noticed that she was talking to me. Suddenly, I had trouble hearing her added comments; they were too complimentary. I blushed with embarrassment, but also felt intense pleasure. Unable to hide this odd mixture of emotions, all I could do was acknowledge them and let them show. As many people do, I often have trouble with compliments. During periods when I doubt my accomplishments—my own self-worth actually—I may feel uneasy about positive reactions openly expressed to me. Some may have difficulties handling criticism or negative reactions toward them. Our customary ways of listening and responding to compliments and criticisms offer clues to how we view ourselves.

GIFTS OR BARTERS?

Our compliments may be given freely, or they may carry conditions that the recipient return the "favor" or live up to other expectations and demands implied. Compliments given with strings attached become barters. At work Gloria intentionally and almost promiscuously showered compliments on others, hoping that her bouquets would boomerang. Later she acknowledged that she needed to hear good things about herself, as she put it, "to bolster my sagging ego." Her approach backfired. Instead of getting the positive reactions she so much wanted, she drew suspicious ones. Friends finally told her, "You seem unreal"; "You come through as Pollyanna." Gloria's need for support stemmed from her belief that she was too fragile to handle negative reactions to her. The criticism hurt, but she finally listened and felt less fragile. She gained more credibility in the eyes of others, and, more importantly, in her own eyes. She needed to learn to give more discriminating responses to others and to deepen and enrich the quality of her relationships.

Alan, a seminary student, also wanted people to react positively toward him. He needed others to enhance his self-esteem, yet he devalued what others said. He once acknowledged, "I feel like a fraud and want to shout, 'I'm not the person who deserves all these nice things.'" He was on a treadmill, needing and wanting others to value him, yet unable to believe them. Alan's friend and fellow student, Clay, thought that he, too, wanted very much to be complimented. In private, he imagined himself cherishing the compliments. In public, positive remarks from others left him feeling, "If you knew the truth about me you would not say that." He was fearful of being prized too much by others. "That would obligate me to be more open, and that would increase my vulnerability," he said. Rather than trying openly to accept positive reactions, he often subtly denied or ignored them with silence and the safety of feigned humility.

Compliments for which we have angled by showing our need or our complimentary side are seldom believed. We may distrust either the way we get them or the person who gives them.

We may toss compliments aside so deftly that we hardly allow them to touch us. In a human relations workshop a student told a faculty member that he liked and appreciated his compassion for students and his attention to their personal problems. In an even tone, with eyes toward the floor, and an expressionless face, the faculty member replied, "It's just a part of my job." The way he parried the compliment was played back to him by the workshop consultant, who then asked that he try to acknowledge and accept it simply while looking at the student. The faculty member was mildly astonished at the difficulty of the task. He also was both embarrassed and pleased by his game tries and the good-humored support given by other faculty members and students in the group.

Difficulties with such gestures of acceptance that are exceedingly simple on the surface may be rooted in deeper feelings about what we are like and how we "should" respond publicly to approbation. Compliments

37

expressed freely, without strings, are a gift. The person who can hear, acknowledge, and accept such a gift, and prize himself as well as the giver, has enhanced the gift, the giver, and himself.

USES OF CRITICISM

While some of us have a tendency to disbelieve or to minimize the good things people say about us, others among us have a tendency to hold a protective web around ourselves in defense against criticism. One workshop participant said, "I confuse the issue by getting logical in the face of threatening reactions. Sometimes I act helpless so others will stop the criticism." Early in the workshop experience he had received more negative than positive reactions. While he was fearful of criticism, he found that he had courted it, hoping that he could learn how to handle it and overcome his fear.

We may court negative reactions for other reasons. A therapy group member regarded criticism as more useful than compliments, and criticism is what he often got— not because he asked for it directly, but because of his detached manner, as though he were sitting in judgment of others. Moreover, his tendency to qualify and hedge his opinions and feelings until they had no meaning often brought down the ire of others upon him. He gave the impression of accepting their displeasure stoically, as though it strengthened him. He never openly criticized other members, however.

Still another member, who claimed that "criticism is the stuff that we grow on," gave others criticism galore so they could improve and, in his words, "not appear in a negative light in the future." This member came across as using his ostensible concern for the growth of others as an excuse to criticize and attack them.

Marya, a brilliant graduate student in her early twenties who came for consultation, insisted that she could improve only with criticism. Her reasoning was that she knew the good qualities but that she did not know the bad ones. To have more knowledge of her negative qualities, she believed, would add to her self-understanding and thus enable her to see herself more completely. Marya, in effect, refused to acknowledge and to understand her strengths. She had assembled detailed lists of her negative qualities which she used daily to support an extremely negative view of herself. But they were either exaggerated or unreal.

Despite her attractiveness to others, she convinced herself that she was ugly. When her family bought her new and well-designed articles of clothing (she seldom bought any herself), she left them hanging in the closet for weeks before wearing them once. When someone complimented her on what she wore and asked whether it was new, she could honestly answer no. She did not "deserve" to wear new clothes. She could not bear the pain of hearing compliments, of seeing herself as intelligent, pretty, or worthwhile.

As a child, Marya had received little or no criticism from her parents. She was prized by them. Their major disappointment in her apparently was that she often rejected their overtures of kindness and appreciation, not in anger but in embarrassment, as though she were undeserving. This seemingly mild-mannered young woman, exceptionally courteous and considerate to others, held onto her own negative self-judgment with tenacity. Finally, friends and interested faculty members quit acceding to her persuasive requests for criticism that they could not honestly give. Instead, they gently but firmly confronted her with her own blindness to what she truly was like. Gradually, some of the fear behind her barricade of inadequacy crept through. As it emerged, she felt terrorized at the prospect of facing and acknowledging her own adequacy. She felt certain that it would destroy her, for she could never live up to the demonic perfectionistic expectations that were embedded deeply within. In guarded desperation, she had held her fear at bay for years through feeling unworthy. Now the fear was getting loose. She was on the edge of a new and different battle with herself—more frightening perhaps, but also better understood and more in the open in terms of what the antagonists were like.

Months later a sign of her growth was revealed in a simple though salient exchange. Marya came bouncing into a graduate seminar looking more attractive than usual, wearing a dress we had not seen before. There was a moment of quiet before one of the other women in the seminar observed with friendly interest, "That must be a new dress, Marya; I haven't seen it before." Marya smiled and answered softly, "Yes, it is. Do you like it?"

As children, many of us got a great deal of criticism and, as a result, learned a variety of patterns for coping with it. Marya had apparently received little criticism, but, knowing that she was not perfect and deserved what other children got, developed her own patterns of self-judgment and censure. Being judged, whether we are underestimated or overestimated, usually implies a demand, subtle or direct, that we change. If others do not demand change, we may feel the need to demand it of ourselves.

Reactions that are relatively free from attempts to

change or discredit us, given by someone who cares for us, and with the intention of letting us know what impressions we are making, may be easier to take. If, however, our usual reaction is to defend ourselves, even mild criticism or impressions given gently without demands that we change may play havoc with our defensive structure and become difficult to handle. Marya, for example, had mastered ways of handling negative reactions that fit her self-image. She defended herself against positive reactions by denying or disregarding them. When, however, she was confronted considerately but unequivocally, with mildly negative reactions to her own distorted views of herself, her usual pattern of absorbing the negative was no longer appropriate. She began to adjust her usual ways of dealing with both criticism and compliments and to let in new, more positive perceptions of her behavior that could lead to new self-perceptions and change.

PROTECTING OURSELVES OR OTHERS?

It is not uncommon for us to withhold our reactions to others. We may hold back compliments for fear of embarrassment to them and to ourselves. We may hold back criticism for fear of being disliked or considered unfair, or for fear of hurting another person. Reactions given inconsiderately may indeed hurt others. On the other hand, some of us are inclined to withhold our reactions from others while at the same time we honestly prefer that they not hold back theirs from us. We may have two different rules. The first one may be: If we ask others for candid reactions to our behavior, to something we have done or plan to do, we want them to tell us straight, including the negative with the positive. The second rule may be: If someone else asks us for similar reactions, we are inclined to hold back or gloss over the negative and embroider the positive. For us to act repeatedly on these two rules implies that we can take it and that others cannot, that we are strong and that others are weak, that we can hurt them, but that they cannot hurt us. For us to deny to others what we want or need for ourselves, honest reactions, for instance, may be to undermine others in their strength for handling give-and-take relationships.

But how does one decide when and how to react to someone who has always been handled with kid gloves? Or to someone who feels excessively criticized? The decision of whether or not to withhold reactions is sometimes tricky. When I saw Dan during one individual therapy session he expressed feelings of dependence and helplessness. He was convinced that criticisms from his mother, from his wife (who had left him recently), and now from his boss, had reduced his self-esteem beyond recovery. Yet he came to me with this request: "You criticize me so that I can become a better person." For me to join in such a venture might satisfy Dan's consistently low regard for himself, and at the same time help to maintain it. It was understandable that he often spoke in a whining, self-pitying voice. It was in such tones that he asked plaintively, "I wonder why it is so hard for people to like me?" I needed a moment for courage to tell him with some compassion that I too was having a difficult struggle trying to like him. When I told him what there was about his behavior that made liking him difficult for me, he showed visible relief.

He had faced something which he feared would devastate him, and when he discovered that he could take it and perhaps could change, that gave him hope. To overprotect Dan by sparing him my forthright reaction would have put my own need for self-protection ahead of his need for a straight answer. Moreover, for me to minimize my response would confirm his belief that he was weak and might be annihilated by reactions which he already dimly suspected.

USING BOTH

Regardless of cause, we may have difficulty accepting openly and without qualification many of our positive characteristics. We may have trouble acknowledging that we are lovable, or that we have talents, skills, and personal characteristics that deserve to be recognized and valued. As already indicated, a frequent belief that may accompany our reluctance to acknowledge and appreciate positive qualities is: "While I am pleased to know the good things you see in me, I am more likely to improve myself and to change through hearing and understanding the worst that you see in me."

But even when one has made such a claim, negative reactions are not easily considered, thoughtfully evaluated, and applied to oneself either. As was the case with Marya and with Dan, we may use the negative to nourish our own protective negative views of ourselves. We may show our negative side in the hope that if we are seen at our worst, positive reactions that others may feel toward us will be more trustworthy. We may court negative reactions and use them as justification for lashing back with our own anger and criticism of others. Ideally, we can use negative reactions in sorting out and learning to discriminate between appropriate and inappropriate ways of behaving.

Compliments and criticism are the coin of the realm in many of our relationships. While the ways we give and receive them may seem random, they usually add up to patterns. Some patterns are enhancing to our personal growth and others are defeating. We may, for example, court negative reactions in the belief that criticism strengthens us and that compliments weaken us or do not help us to grow. On the other hand, we may seek compliments in the belief that the positive nourishes us and that the negative stunts us.

For many of us a difficult but necessary task is to learn to listen to both positive and negative impressions and to discover the distortions in them. An equally important task is to learn to give both positive and negative impressions that others may be able to hear and to use. Impressions given altruistically and with clear intent to respect and value the integrity of others are more likely to have credibility and impact. Reactions given in anger, to punish, or to demand change are more likely to devaluate and diminish us.

3. The Feel
of Influence

If I knew . . . that a man was coming to my house with the conscious design of doing me good, I should run for my life.

Henry David Thoreau

Having influence with myself and with other people is an important ingredient in maintaining my self-esteem. Whether in social relationships or the workaday world, I need and seek influence in my relationships. Feeling influential adds to my ability to present myself to others with genuineness and satisfaction. My ability to listen to others sensitively may be the beginning of their trust in me and their willingness for me to have influence in their lives. Similarly, I am more inclined to entrust others with influence if they truly hear me.

WHO HAS INFLUENCE?

It is common knowledge that we listen to others and allow them to have sway over us according to how we feel about them and want them to feel about us. The opinions and reactions of people we like and value and of those who like and value us, for instance, are likely to be heard and to carry weight. But recognizing the kinds of influence we allow each other to have is not a simple matter. If I have too much need for your respect, I may be afraid to risk losing it by letting you know some of the ways I feel and act. Similarly, if I like someone a great deal and give a great deal of weight to his reactions, the thought of what his response might be could frighten me and make hearing him difficult.

With a high-status person, we may have trouble telling the difference between those reactions that are useful and those that we judge important because of the person's importance. If someone is prestigious, we may attach too much importance to what he says because we want to please, to show respect, or because we feel dependent. If we are fearful or disapprove of our dependence, we may try to deny our attitude by ignoring or discrediting what he says. Thus, some of us may be inappropriately influenced by high-status persons by attaching too much or too little importance to their views.

We may attach special significance to other people's reactions to us because of such things as their age, sex, religion, or manner of dress, depending on how we have come to see them. For instance, Gene, a first-year graduate student, regarded men's reactions to him in the pastoral counseling workshop as more valid and important than women's. "Men are not so easily fooled by me and are more likely than women to see the way I really am," he said. Gene worked hard to impress women, much harder than he did to impress men; then he ended up not believing their usually favorable reactions to him. In his eyes, he had gotten their positive responses fraudulently. Further, he discovered that he regarded few women as equals and, consequently, did not value their reactions to him, positive or negative. Since he did see some older women as equals, he attached more value to what they said. In a series of role-playing situations others acted out ways they saw Gene behaving toward women. He was shocked to discover the depth and extent of his prejudices.

If we feel another person's opinions of us to be so important that we take them as "the truth" and try to change to fit that person's picture, he may no longer be free to say what he thinks and feels about us. Tom needed so much from others that he could not use what they gave. He diligently sought the opinions of those around him and seemed obsessed with attempting to be whatever he thought they wanted him to be. He succeeded in pleasing neither them nor himself. His efforts to give others excessive influence over his life led them to give up trying to have any.

On the other side of the coin, if nothing we say or do seems to make the slightest impact on others, the futility of our efforts also may lead us to quit trying to make contact with them. Giving reactions to Jerry, even when he asked for them, was like shouting down an echoless canyon. Nothing ever came back. Friends and associates seldom knew whether or not Jerry heard or was influenced by them. He seemed impenetrable. As a consequence, people around him made fewer and fewer comments that had significance either to him or to them. Also because of his armor and lack of responsiveness, he occasionally became the target of the frustrations and anger of some associates. They discovered that they could vent their anger on him without the danger that he would respond and have to be faced. So his inner isolation and lack of self-worth were increased.

We also grant others influence according to the *ways*

they talk and relate to us. We look and listen for signs indicating that they value us. In contrast, we may pick up signals indicating that they are patronizing and critical in ways that leave us feeling pushed away and punished. In our distrust we may ask ourselves questions: Are their reactions and what they offer in a relationship freely given? Are they covertly asking for something in return? Does their behavior toward us seem to be free from deception, tricks, gimmicks? But seldom do we voice these questions.

And after a while we may become so accustomed to disguising our feelings that we no longer know precisely what they are. Still, we may detect clearly the disguises others use. If I express a concern of mine to someone, he may listen sensitively and compassionately and show it in a way that dignifies me and my feelings. Or, in the guise of support, he may respond in ways that minimize and discredit me in a patronizing manner, like giving a child a pat on the head and telling him "There, there—it will work itself out." I probably will have little difficulty sensing his response to me although I may not understand it fully. Giving impressions without garnish, sometimes referred to as telling it straight, may be hostility in disguise. The person who says to me, "I must be perfectly honest and tell you what I think about you, no matter what" is likely to put me on guard. It is difficult for me to believe that he is out to do me good. As a result, what he says is unlikely to have much influence with me.

LISTENING AS A WELLSPRING OF INFLUENCE

Over and over again, I encounter what seems to me to be a paradox in my attempts to have influence with other people. With family, friends, students, and people I see in therapy, I seem to have more influence when I do not need or want it. And I seem to have less when I try to get and use it. If I can listen, understand, remain relatively nonjudgmental, and care about people with whom I am in frequent and close contact, they often hear and value what I have to say. Having heard them, I am more free to express my reactions in a straightforward manner. My reactions may have impact, though I may not know the degree or the direction of it. If, however, I listen and respond in a way that suggests that I have a sizable investment in the direction my influence takes, I may lose influence. Although I understand how this process of having and not having influence occurs, I am not always able to make use of that knowledge. Sometimes I still get so inextricably involved with others, particularly members of my family, that I begin to act as though I know too much about what is best for them. I become too possessive and show too little faith and trust in their ability to take greater responsibility for themselves. Usually at this point I have to work to sort out my needs from theirs to become clear about what I am doing.

I react similarly in a negative fashion to other people who try to exert too much influence on me. I am more willing to listen and to consider seriously what another person says to me, and may even want to change, if that person has no stake in changing me. By giving me his reactions and some sign of acceptance, he may bolster me enough to try new behavior. If I feel pushed to change, I may try, but I also may dig in and defend against doing so, even though I really do not like the way I am. Then again, if someone is especially important to me and needs for me to change, I may want so much to please him that I show superficial signs of change. At some level I may be pushing him away, escaping him through superficial

51

compliance. Also, I may resent him for rejecting me as I am. Most likely, however, I will resent myself for being so unacceptable to him and so lacking in confidence that I cannot accept myself despite him.

INFLUENCE LOST, THEN FOUND

Occasionally we may get so caught up in our own misery and unacceptable thoughts that we feel powerless to change. We may feel unable to listen to ourselves and others and to use the responses and relationships they offer. Lacking influence with ourselves and lagging in self-esteem, we may feel lost and depressed. Try as we may to reach out to others so they might touch us to revive our spirits, we flounder. Finally, we may wonder: Is there any hope? Who can help, have influence when our own hope seems lost? An experience with Maury illustrates.

Maury was in a "poor me" state, unable to use support and understanding offered by others even though he was starving for human contact. In his own words, "I often languish on the edge of a group of people waiting for someone to say something nice to me, but it seldom comes. Then I decide to make myself better by liking me more, but that doesn't work either. Even when people are nice to me, I can't believe it, don't deserve it, since I have not done anything to earn it. I get sad, depressed, and physically sick waiting for someone to come and say good things. So, in a room full of people, I'm scared, want to get out, don't trust, don't feel liked. What can I do? Can I do anything? I want something, but I've asked for too much and have done too little to get it. . . ."

Maury was on a merry-go-round. He would sit sadly or dourly at the edge of the therapy group until someone tried to draw him into the discussion. Karen once ·confronted him: "You make a complaint, bring up a gripe, or tell us a problem, and sit back as though you are waiting for us to take it over from you and solve it. I try to stay with you, to get involved with you, but you run away. You weasel out and then blame us for not paying attention to you, or feel sorry for yourself as though you are trying so hard and we ignore you."

Maury answered helplessly, "I don't know what else to do besides tell you what's bothering me."

Lynn angrily told Maury, "You remind me of a dump truck driving up to someone, dumping your load of garbage and then driving off before anyone can do anything with it."

Maury responded in a high-pitched voice and with a look of hurt, "Then why don't you help me do something?" With that plea he had dumped another load.

Some of Maury's friends and the members of the therapy group became frustrated with his helplessness and his rejection of their overtures and began to tune him out. One night, after six or seven hours in a long therapy group session, Maury made a last-ditch stand to express his frustrations and anger over being ignored. I invited him to stand (a soapbox stance) and tell people in the group how inconsiderate, unkind, and callous he thought they were. He waved his arms and went through the motions of expressing anger, but his search for a crowning achievement failed. He moved quietly to a corner and wilted. People in the group felt crushed and guilty for the failure but moved on to other things. Maury was ignored again.

Later in the evening, we were in the Magic Shop, a psychological bartering experience in which participants seek psychological wares and pay prices in terms of risks in trying new behavior. Again, Maury was on the fringe. After two or three transactions with other members, I happened to glance at Maury sitting expectantly on the edge of the circle. Spontaneously, I invited him to take over the Magic Shop, and I moved out of the scene. Maury came alive. He moved into the center of the room, not at all in need, not begging, not helpless, not apologetic, much in contrast to his sulking withdrawal to the corner.

Glancing around the room, he saw Howard sitting against the wall, on the fringe of the group near where he had been. Howard often had given the image of a frightened and helpless person who covered his helplessness and dependence with anger that flared at the slightest provocation. Apparently sensing an affinity for Howard, Maury moved in front of him and, with a mixture of softness, lightness, and unexpected force, said, "Howard, you're a PMS (poor miserable slob) just like I am, so I want to invite you to the Magic Shop."

Both Maury and Howard moved to the center of the room. After a few minutes of negotiation they agreed that Howard should seek assertiveness and independence in the Magic Shop as a way to increase his self-esteem. A part of the price that he had to pay was to go around the room and tell members that he once was a PMS but now is a person with considerable poise, confidence, and ability.

Howard began his task. When he faltered Maury coached him. Both caricatured themselves and one another, first as poor miserable slobs, then as self-confident young men who had completely reformed themselves. Their act drew such a crescendo of hilarity that the entire group soon broke into spontaneous applause.

Maury was exuberant. With authority conferred upon him, he assumed it and conferred it upon Howard. In taking on some responsibility for the group, he took more responsibility for himself. In assisting Howard in asserting himself, Maury became more assertive. The playfulness and the zany, gamelike quality of the situation allowed plenty of room for trying different kinds of behavior; it allowed both for failure and for success that did not need to be too obvious or taken too seriously. Yet underneath, no one in the room could doubt that this was a serious experience both for Maury and Howard, but especially for Maury.

For the remainder of the session, Maury was direct in his confrontation of others; playful, warm, and sensitive. He took risks freely. The entire therapy group came alive with excitement. In Maury's words at a later session, "I felt ecstatic; I was giving and receiving and had hit the jackpot. I desperately wanted and needed responsibility, to take initiative on my own and to focus on others for a while, and then come back to me. The rest of the night is a series of flashes, the largest and brightest of which are the things I heard that I wanted and needed to hear so long. People said, 'You are beautiful,' and that was great. I was feeling free. A dam had broken and I was no longer afraid of myself or of the other people there. I was real in my actions. Then for the next few days I became painfully aware of the earlier feelings of being outside and uncared for and of the contrast with the sensation of belonging and of being cared for."

Maury had lost power over himself and influence with others. With the loss of influence and his self-worth he had become frightened and closed himself off to others, was unable to hear them at a time he desperately needed them. Members of the group, frustrated with their own powerlessness to help, had withdrawn in frustration. When Maury had finally snatched his chance, he reestablished relationships almost spontaneously. He seemed to experience truth in the old biblical suggestion that we must lose ourselves to find ourselves. Somewhere from within him emerged sufficient freedom, perhaps abandon, to risk showing his own adequacy and influence in asserting himself as a separate person who could make contact with others.

As Maury felt his influence over himself, with Howard, and in the group, he seemed more able to listen to others and to allow them to have influence with him. As he sensed autonomy and independence, he seemed also to sense that being separate is a part of what one person has to offer in relationships with others. Once Maury had convinced himself and members of the group that no one could help, he discovered that someone, in fact he himself, could.

Powerlessness can have a numbing effect and can shut us down psychologically. Having fluctuating degrees of influence in a variety of relationships and our daily environment is a means of developing a belief in our own worth and the worth of others. We are likely to be seen as influential and as creditable when we appear to have influence over our own lives. We may be entrusted with influence when we are more altruistic than self-centered and more open than guarded. Influence may come when we can listen in ways that demonstrate our respect for the integrity and separateness of others.

4. Barriers to Listening

"Before I built a wall I'd ask to know
  What I was walling in or walling out,
And to whom I was like to give offense.
  Something there is that doesn't love a wall,
That wants it down."

Robert Frost

Listening and hearing in sensitive ways are open mine shafts to understanding and to an infinite variety of pleasing human relationships. Yet our potential for focused and sensitive listening often remains embedded within us, raw and unrefined, like a rich lode of unmined ore. Our views and understanding of one another also can become distorted when our listening gets cluttered and blocked by the prejudices we bring out of our past, and by the myriad of emotional barriers and biases in our day-to-day relationships. This chapter discusses common emotional barriers to our listening; the next describes unexamined biases that intrude upon the ways we listen.

WHY WE TUNE OUT

When we find ourselves not listening, we may be bored, tired, in a hurry, or we may have one of a dozen other simple reasons for tuning out. Barriers to our listening, however, may be more complex, perhaps subtle—something going on inside us. The actual task of trying to discover why we have listening barriers can be profitable, but also discouraging when improvement comes slowly, if at all. I am referring to occasions when we *want* and *need* to be listening, or at least think we should, rather than to those occasions when we *choose not* to listen well.

SEPARATING OURSELVES FROM OTHERS

I have trouble listening to others when my emotional involvement reaches the point where I am unable to separate myself from them. I can sometimes listen to the problems of other people's children easier than I can to those of my own. Unfortunately, I sometimes regard my children as an extension of myself and may not clearly separate them from myself. My emotional involvement blinds me. I may be less tolerant of their behavior and less attentive, for example, when I become overly concerned with what others might think of their behavior and, as a result, of me. On the other hand, sometimes I have trouble listening to them when I blame myself for causing their concerns. My emotional involvement with them may show itself in other ways which keep me from hearing them clearly—excessive criticism, restricting their behavior unduly, or overprotecting them.

My unavailability or inattentive listening was vividly called to my attention by my younger daughter, age eleven at the time. She wrote me a telling note inquiring about the possibility of an appointment to talk with me about an "important personal matter." My limited accessibility was underscored a few weeks later by my older teenage daughter. After sharing some boyfriend problems and situations with me, she gently slipped her arm in mine as we walked from my study and said appreciatively, with a touch of both jest and seriousness, "Thanks. Just send me the bill."

If when I care the most, I listen the least, my listening does not show much caring.

Another block to listening may be our own current inner struggles. Listening to someone else may trigger feelings about similar problems or concerns that we are facing or unexpectedly lead us to question ourselves. The other day I was listening to Angie, a seventeen-year-old girl, as she tearfully expressed the belief that her father seemed never to listen to what she had to say. "Mostly," she said, "he ignores what I say and then criticizes me." At first I could listen freely. Then, for a few seconds, I noticed that I was torn between listening to her and wondering how I had been listening to my own children lately. "Not too badly," was my inner reply. With this satisfactory, though tentative, progress report I was able to quit listening to myself and get back to Angie.

Our conflicts may be so much like another person's that we have difficulty extricating our concerns from theirs as we listen. Miriam was sharing her identification with Sandy during an experience in their therapy group. "I seemed very aware of her when she was restless, daydreaming, discontent," Miriam recalled. "I can picture Sandy sitting in the center of the room. I listened to her as she talked about her boyfriend and wanting to get married and her conflicting feelings over wanting to be a grown woman but also wanting to be a little girl again.

She was talking about being a little girl back home. Suddenly I was sitting in the garden in my backyard, bored, but somehow content, aimlessly digging up dirt with a stick. I was waiting for my daddy to come home. I heard her words, but it was my voice. She (I) was suddenly an uncertain little girl facing her (my) father instead of a young woman facing her lover. The woman in her demanded that the child retreat, and Sandy was in confusion. I understood her completely. I was *there*. Immediately I realized that the I-her between me and Sandy had become I-I. How strange! I was hearing the little girl side of me trying to cope with a confusing situation. Gradually my confusion subsided as I thought about my little girl side and how I enjoy and use her sometimes."

Miriam identified with Sandy as she listened. Her feelings then became almost indistinguishable from Sandy's. When her own experiences came so completely into focus that she began hearing only herself, she became unable to hear anyone else.

CAUGHT IN A WEB OF EMOTIONS

Our hearing can be impaired also when we fear that we may get caught in some unknown web of emotion. We may become cautious, guarded, or carried away with our own feelings. Our listening is blocked, whether our emotions are touched off by what the other person is saying or by the feelings we bring.

Gina, a member of a therapy group, was listening to Mark express in agonizing words his guilt and fear over leaving his wife of ten years. He had gone, in his own eyes, from being a younger boy just out of his teens in his mother's home to being an older boy in his twenties in his wife's home. Now, in despair he said, "I don't know whether I'm a man, or a boy who can't survive without a constant mother." Mark was sitting on the floor shifting nervously. Gina, sitting a few feet across the room, watched him intently, nodded understandingly, then noted softly, "But there are so many good things about you that you're just not looking at." She paused and suddenly shouted in exasperation, "Why don't you look at them, Mark? Why don't you look at them?" Mark gazed at her and continued to talk, more to himself than to Gina, "When you're driving and you can't tell the road from the trees, yourself from the car, don't know where you've been and where you're going and don't care, it's time to do something. I have to change my life. It's all wrong."

Mark was staring at the floor, moving his body now in a rocking motion. Gina, who continued to look at him, was stroking her thighs with the palms of her hands, unaware of her movements. In a monotone she said, "It all needs to be smoothed out, smoothed out. It can be . . . (pause) . . . that's what my own little boy needs when he is hurt and scared." Gina's own world had engulfed her; she had lost touch with Mark. An hour or more later she remembered her panic one night three years back. Her son, then two, went into convulsions while the two of them were waiting, the only passengers, in the bus station of a small western town. While listening to Mark her fear from that night had reappeared. After experiencing her fear and its connection with her son, she was accessible to listen to Mark, even in his most boyish moments, with less of a barrier. But while she was involved with her own fear, she could not hear Mark as a separate person.

Can you recall a recent experience in which you listened to someone and felt so overcome with emotions that you could hardly hear? You may have felt anger, hurt, fear, joy. Your emotions may have taken off in their own direction or may have paralleled those of the person to whom you were listening. Someone else's tears may have become your tears; his or her anger, your anger.

A few years back I was working with a therapy training group. A young woman whose father had died two years earlier was, through a fantasy experience, trying to talk to him, to express some feelings that troubled her. She pictured herself at his graveside and began to talk. She could not speak beyond saying "Dad." Her eyes were closed. She was asked if she would like for someone from the group to be her father. Maybe it would help if her father could speak back. She asked me to do that. With her eyes closed she told her father how much she missed him and how sorry she was for the times she had neglected him. She shared the guilt that she had been feeling and that was burdening her now. She also told him, as she sobbed softly, that she had appreciated him more than she had ever told him. There were so many things that she wanted to say!

I responded understandingly as her father, maybe as I would want to respond as a father. In experiencing and responding to her tears of grief, I got caught deeply in my own tears, my own grief, possibly for myself as a father or for my own father. I am not sure. Suddenly, all I could do was weep with her. We sat on the floor holding one another, weeping tears too deep for words.

In a way I had failed her, had gotten too caught up in my own emotions. In still another way I had listened so deeply that I met her at the core of her grief with my own. We both stayed there for awhile. Finally, we could talk to one another about what we felt. She could hear me and I began to hear her again, both free from the emotions now.

I saw her this summer. She remembered the experience. Her face was alive with joy as she said, "I really was able to get my feelings about my father straight, no hangover, no guilt."

She had been touched through being heard. I had been touched too. She had put me in touch with sorrow that I had entombed. We had begun with only one of us being a caring listener. Having heard one another in moments of grief, both of us then became caring listeners—caring but separate.

EXPECTATIONS AND DAILY EVENTS AS BARRIERS

Almost every day someone's expectations of me may become a barrier to my listening. If, for instance, someone wants to be closer in the relationship than I prefer, I may be guarded and cautious and miss much of what he or she expresses. Sometimes my overconcern and self-doubt about whether or not I can make a difference in the lives of people who seek relief from their conflicts day after day can cripple my ability to listen. My need to give too much or the fear that I can offer too little can be impediments. I must confront myself to reexamine what I *can* and *cannot* truly bring to the experience of listening to another person.

When I feel threatened or experience dislike for another person, I may not listen openly or carefully. If I resent someone without an acceptable reason, I may feel guilty for not meeting my own expectation that I should like other people. As a result I may resent myself for such an unjustified feeling. I may then double my listening efforts to make up for my guilt. Now I am in a double bind—resentful and guilty, striving to listen harder to compensate, but succeeding only in exaggerating my failure to listen.

Certain rather ordinary events can precipitate barriers to listening and distort what we hear. If my day has been satisfying, the ring of my phone may signal that a friend I want to hear is calling. If my day has been burdensome and frustrating, the ring of the phone may sound like one more bothersome problem. Connie, who works for a research organization, had just gotten home from conducting a door-to-door attitude survey. "I was totally wrung out; it had been a terrible, terrible afternoon," she said the next day. "The phone rang and it was Byrne, my boyfriend, checking to see if he could bring over anything for the dinner we had planned to fix. I said, 'No, but would you mind picking up some cigarettes for me?' 'Yes, I do mind,' Byrne replied, 'I wish you wouldn't start to smoke again and I don't want to help you do it.'" Connie continued, "I hung up and started crying; it was just one more door slammed in my face. An hour later I could recall that his voice had been gentle, and that there was concern and caring for me in what he was saying. But the earlier events of my day had screened out my ability to hear his caring."

BARRIERS IN OTHERS

The obstacles we encounter in listening and understanding often are within ourselves. But sometimes they stem from the behavior of others. When a person fails to listen to himself as he talks, I too may be disinclined to want to hear. Cy spoke in a low, constant monotone. The only evidence that he might be checking for contact with other members of the seminar discussion group was that he occasionally raised his eyes and glanced at someone.

Was he checking to be certain that no one was listening, or that someone was? Later, I found out that he was doing both. He wanted to be heard, but half-heartedly wanted to be ignored. The way he spoke represented his conflict. He felt a compelling desire to trust others and to let himself become more known. He also felt distrust and fear that others would dislike him if he exposed his wide-ranging beliefs and feelings. Later, when we understood Cy's conflict, it was easier to listen to him, but he needed to remove the façade of disinterest in himself and to risk the consequences of how others might respond if he wanted to be heard.

Do you ever speak so softly that others can hardly hear you? When you do speak softly, do you want to be sure that someone pays special attention? Or, are you uncertain about whether or not you want to be heard? Maybe you are unaware of whether or not your voice volume is too low for others to hear. Speaking too softly may be a barrier to being heard. Speaking too loudly also may be a way of being unheard. The meaning may get lost in the sound. An experience with Ward illustrates.

In an intensive small group which was part of a larger human relations workshop, Ward's excessive and inappropriate use of four-letter words carried the tones and evocative challenge of anger, but Ward smiled a lot as he talked. His words and his boisterous, braggadocio manner in the dimly lit, carpeted, well-furnished room seemed to say louder than necessary, "Look at me." But what did Ward want us to see? When in his turbulence and urgency, he released his gutsy feelings, they reminded me of a huge boulder cascading down the mountain at the onset of a rock slide. At other times Ward was like a huge Saint Bernard puppy romping over the room and the people in it, attempting to give and to receive affection, but finding

67

instead that others were unready and unable to respond on his terms.

Where do we begin to listen to Ward and to people who, like him, ask in loud but camouflaged ways to be heard? We found that we could begin by sharing with him why we had trouble listening, and by exploring ways he might express himself differently as we tried to listen anew.

People who speak either too softly or too loudly to be understood often are surprised that their voice levels are not regarded as normal by those around them. They also often are surprised to discover that their voice levels are associated with other behavior that may make listening and understanding them difficult. The meaning of our voice levels and how they are rooted in our emotions and relationships is intriguing and well worth teasing out and understanding.

Voice levels usually carry mixed messages. So may humor, wit, sarcasm, and the variety of emotions that our words and tones may carry. Morris, a young instructor in psychology, conveyed mixed messages when he overly controlled his emotions and his actions.

Morris was bright, knowledgeable about his field, and often likable. He was burdened, however, with the belief that because he knew some psychology he should be able to use his knowledge in maintaining high self-esteem and almost complete self-confidence at all times. He regarded himself as weak when he had self-doubts or experienced conflict and anxiety. When his self-esteem was low, he would cover up by acting even more self-assured, more self-sufficient, and more detached than at other times. His excessive self-control made him seem less natural and less likable.

Morris conveyed two different messages that often became mixed: interest in others, warmth in relationships, and confidence in himself; or the opposite, cool aloofness and an inflexibility that made him seem crisp in relationships. The unpredictable mixtures of his behavior made listening and relating to him difficult. People were uncertain which Morris they would meet and hear.

A barricade to listening may be thrown up by the person who seems completely out of control, whether in anger, sadness, or extreme need. Early in a therapy group, Jennifer broke into deep sobs as she expressed feelings of being hopelessly lost. In effect, before other members of the group could get any feel for her being lost, she was seeking help in being found and in finding herself. No doubt, Jennifer wanted and needed to be heard, but what she wanted others to hear was too much, too soon. She was out of control and the group members were not equipped to cope with her. It was as though her house were engulfed in flames and each person present had at the moment only one small pail of water. Although others could not understand her, they did express their desire to do so. Their willingness helped her to live with her dilemmas until she could express them in ways they could begin to understand.

It seems apparent that these various *barriers* to listening we have just examined are usually traps for the moment that have resulted from a particular problem, person, or circumstance. However, our *biases* in listening are likely to represent patterns that have been developed through the years as the result of our own unique life experiences and the ways we have learned to relate to different people. Listening *biases,* represented in the patterned ways we hear, are more likely to be predictable than *barriers,* which are more specific to different situations and conditions, as we have seen. Barriers also tend to be more transitory than biases. But, as indicated

69

earlier, barriers sometimes result from getting caught up in our own emotions or from having personalities so loosely defined that we cannot separate ourselves and our problems from other people and their problems.

Some of us may maintain somewhat permanent barriers to certain people or particular subjects. We might put up a wall against hearing by characteristically being in a hurry or by becoming anxious or impatient in the face of hearing another person's problems. When this happens, what was originally a barrier develops into a specific bias.

5. Our Built-in Biases

This life's five windows of the soul
* Distorts the Heavens from pole to pole*
And leads you to believe a lie
* When you see with, not thro', the eye.*

William Blake

We listen in different ways to different people, depending on such things as their age, sex, mannerisms, emotional states, or authority in relation to us. Such ways of listening reflect biases—some subtle and disguised, others transparent. People who spend a great deal of time around us, who listen to us, and who watch us listening to them become aware of many of our biases. These are reflected in the different voice tones, facial expressions, body gestures, and the words that we use in response. Our listening biases often are a direct reflection of what we are feeling toward another person and may be more transparent at times than we want them to be.

CHILDREN, ADULTS

Some of us may listen differently to children than to adults. One or the other may be easier to hear. Mona, a social worker in her late twenties, was more comfortable and at home with children. She could listen to a belligerent or whining child with patience and genuine concern. She often seemed uneasy, however, with adults, particularly young men who were her colleagues. To them she listened critically, challenging their statements and engaging them in debate. Mona seemed to identify with children and to project her loving, childlike self in relationships with them. She was likely to project her angry, distrusting self in relationships with men, possibly because she felt that she had been mistreated and abandoned by important men in her life as she grew up. Regardless of causes, some of her listening biases were bound up in the different ways she looked at children and adults, particularly men.

APPEARANCE, SPEECH, MANNER

A person's appearance, words, tone of voice, or mannerisms might affect our listening. Graduate students in psychology have looked askance when asked whether they can listen better to people who have long hair than to those whose hair is short, to students who are barefooted or those who wear shoes when they come for interviews. Later they conducted interviews with people who were highly diverse in manner and appearance and were surprised to discover their listening biases.

Expressions or voice tones that some of us find pleasant and easy to listen to, others may find annoying and difficult to hear. "Cleo has two phrases that really bother me." Glenna complained. "When she says after each sentence, 'See what I mean' or 'Don't you know?' I get disgusted and switch her off." Jack had a gravelly voice. Linda found it irritating; Janet found it soothing.

Tony was sharing a similar experience from a counseling training workshop. "As I walked across the room to get coffee, my back was to Lon, who began to talk. I was filling my cup when I suddenly realized that Lon's voice was annoying me with its jerky whine. I was shocked to discover this; I liked Lon. Why hadn't I noticed it before? And why did I notice it now that I was listening but not seeing him? I returned to my seat, still trying to figure out why I had not noticed Lon's voice before. After a couple of minutes I observed that Lon talks a lot with his hands. They draw my attention from his voice and sort of punctuate what he means. His face and hands filter out the annoying tone of his voice for me."

EMOTIONAL EXPRESSIONS

So many different people enter our world of listening that we may have difficulty sorting out our biases as we hear them express different feelings—joy or sorrow, pleasure or pain, laughter or tears. Some people may listen to sadness and feel compassion and understanding for the person expressing it. Others may withdraw in fright. Still others may find that hearing sadness triggers their own and makes them react aggressively. Jesse, a professional man in his mid-thirties who had never married, usually responded to children with warmth, compassion, and sensitivity. He had a special sense for knowing what they were feeling and an uncanny ability to enter their world of play. When children were sad, however, it was another story. Unable to listen to them, Jesse withdrew, caught up perhaps in his own sadness.

MALE, FEMALE

For some of us, the sex of the person expressing a feeling makes a difference in how we listen. Some men have

75

far more tolerance and ability for listening openly to women weep than to other men. But others take unusual steps to keep women from crying. There are exceptions, of course, but women often seem to me to be more tolerant than men in allowing and listening to other adults cry.

I am sometimes more patient and accepting in listening to women than to men in therapy sessions. Occasionally, I may feel a bit more demanding of men because of the demands I place on myself. I discover that as I become more tolerant and less critical of myself, I am more open and receptive to the expression of a wider range of emotions by men.

Arnie flared in angry denial when Doreen told him that his analysis of her behavior in the group made her feel like a specimen under a microscope rather than a person. Yet Arnie had thanked a man for a similar reaction earlier and regarded it as helpful. That Arnie listened differently to potentially critical remarks from women than to those from men was made quite evident to him. But for some men, the opposite is true. Criticism from women is easier to hear.

PARENTS, CHILDREN

As parents, our feelings of responsibility and attitudes toward others in our family affect our listening. We may characteristically listen to our children with feelings of trust or with skepticism, questioning what they say. We may sometimes simply refuse to listen. A mother of three daughters was usually open to anything they wanted to talk to her about. She kindly but consistently refused, however, to listen and be an arbiter when they sought her support in their squabbles among themselves. Her standard line was, "Go work it out yourselves."

Children also vary greatly in their ways of listening to their parents. Bob, a high school senior, admits he often tunes out advice from his parents that he might follow if it came from a friend or a teacher. "I always prejudge what they say. I expect them to say something that I don't want to hear." Bob paused, adding, "It bothers me once in a while that I may miss things that they tell me that I could use." Tim's set was different. He usually listened to his parents, because he said, "I don't always have to do what they say."

Kathy, now twenty-two and out of college, is struggling with a new way of listening to her parents. "I have become aware recently that I have the hardest time when they talk to me as 'regular people' and not as parents. I have a hard time listening when they share their problems with me. In many ways I insist on remaining their child. But when they talk to me about their problems I have to be more grown up with them." Kathy continued, laughing at herself, "It's funny that I feel this way because most of the time I can't stand for them to treat me as their little girl. But I still can't seem to accept the fact that my parents are ordinary people who have worries like other adults." She frowned as though something new had just occurred to her. "Yes," she added firmly, "I do resent their talking to me that way and my having to try to listen to them." Her parents can help her remain immature by shielding her or perhaps help her to grow by continuing to talk to her as an adult on many occasions. For Kathy and her parents to share openly what is bothersome to listen to and what is not can clear the air and help to keep the listening lines open.

Parents often are acutely aware of the biased ways their children select what they want to hear. Selective listening is biased; it is hearing what we consciously or unconsciously choose to hear. My wife called from the kitchen to our two daughters and son in their rooms, "Will you children come and set the table and help with dinner?" No reply was heard. Were they listening? Was her voice loud enough to be heard? Within a few minutes she asked me in a voice lower than before, "What color telephone do the children want?" Almost in unison the reply came from the three children in their rooms: "Yellow."

UP, DOWN, ACROSS

We may be inclined to listen differently to someone over whom we have considerable influence, to whom we are an expert or an authority, than to someone who might have influence, be an authority over us. Put another way, we might "listen down," when we have influence, differently from the way we "listen up," when someone else has it.

Both Mel and Myra listened to their college professors as though they were absorbing every word, but they were listening differently. Mel was overeager to please, needed to look good, and listened superficially, more concerned with the impression he was making than with what he heard. Myra wanted to know what was being said and was taking it in, weighing it carefully, with little regard for how she looked in the process.

Van, a young junior high teacher, listened down to students as though they needed to be corrected, criticized, and put straight. He fit the stereotype of the army sergeant. In contrast, he listened up to his principal with excessive deference, flattery, and fawning. Judith, an office manager, listened down and up differently. She listened to employees she supervised in a highly protecting, hovering, maternal manner, giving attention to what each had to say. But when her supervisors transacted business with her, she listened belligerently, as though she might shoot from the hip. In both instances, however, in listening down and listening up, Judith sought to dominate and control.

Some people have a happy facility for "listening across" to others, regardless of social or job status and the situation at the moment. We may be more able to listen across when we value ourselves and feel valued by others. With our self-esteem intact we may feel free to be sensitive to others, but not be overly influenced or controlled by them. In listening across we are likely to show a great deal of openness and thoughtfulness to others and to their ideas and feelings, whether we agree or disagree, like or dislike what they say.

OUR CHARACTERISTIC BIASES

As you and I listen to what another person is saying, you may hear good news, and I may hear the bad. You may hear with optimism and I may hear with pessimism. You may hear someone express a dilemma in terms of religious beliefs, and I may hear him in terms of emotional conflict. I may hear him as one more person set upon bothering me with his troubles, and you may hear him as someone who has honored you with trust and the privilege of sharing his life. You may hear what is said in personal terms as a compliment to you, and I may hear the same statement in personal terms as a criticism of me.

While some of us tend to bias our listening by over-personalizing what we hear, others may tend to depersonalize or generalize highly personal statements a person makes. Al, a young man in a long marathon therapy group, was saying, "I sometimes hate my mother when

79

she criticizes and tries to dominate my life." Doris, the mother of a twenty-year-old son, replied with a disapproving tone, "Oh, Al, you don't mean that. No one can hate his mother." Her own needs led her to devalue Al's highly personal statement and to generalize her negation.

During a later session of this marathon, Doris did it again. Jerry said, with sadness in his voice, "Last night I got in touch with my feelings of loneliness and realized that I am not close, really close, to another human being. I had forgotten what it is like to feel love and intimacy." Doris again intervened with, "Everyone feels like that, Jerry. It's just a normal thing, nothing to worry about." Doris' generalizations—"No one hates his mother" and "Everyone feels like that"—depersonalized and minimized what Al and Jerry said and felt.

Our listening attitudes often become patterned so that we hear particular people, ideas, and feelings with characteristic and predictable biases. Children learn early about the right and the wrong times to share bits of news and to make requests from others in the family in order to get the best hearing. When we know the listening attitudes of others we often can predict the best times and places to be heard. We can select conversation topics to fit their needs and ours, and seek reactions that we want, whether a sympathetic and supportive response, a lively give-and-take discussion, agreement, or disagreement. But we may not be as skillful in uncovering our own biases in listening and responding as we are in uncovering those of other people we know.

The stereotypes we assign to other people bias the ways we listen to them characteristically. Stereotypes breed preconceptions of what others *will* say and keep us from hearing fully what they *do* say.

Our stereotypes of others may be based on their

religion, political party, skin color, what they do for a living, how they dress, or where they live. We may, for instance, use age as a basis for stereotyping. Young people, because of presumed differences in beliefs and life styles, may distort how they hear someone who is older. But older people also may set themselves apart and discredit themselves as persons to be heard. Tom, a forty-six-year-old attorney in a seminar whose other members ranged in age from twenty-three to thirty-five, remarked partly in jest, "I feel ancient. Here I am forty-six and a grandfather. I am old and out of place with you young people!" Despite reactions from others indicating that they did not care about his age and wanted to know him for what he was, Tom seemed not to hear. It was weeks later before he could acknowledge his fear of rejection and quit using his age to distance himself. He characteristically assumed that the younger people would hear him with biases associated with his age.

Biases based on stereotypes stem from the fact that we are not listening to others openly as individuals. Instead, we listen to what we expect from people "like them." Whether our stereotype is positive or negative, whether we listen "favorably" or "unfavorably," we are editing and distorting, because we are not allowing those we stereotype to be fully accredited as individuals in our eyes—and ears.

BIASES WE BRING OUT IN OTHERS

We sometimes listen and then respond to particular people in ways that actually *bring out* characteristic behavior patterns from them. Our behavior may constitute a cue for others to talk about certain subjects, to show particular feelings, or to avoid us. Sam's quiet easy manner, his soft voice and open friendly face, seemed to put people at ease. He was seen as an all-around nice guy. When he listened to people around him, they immediately sensed his interest in what they were saying and were eager to share their good news and bad with him. Dudley, in contrast, was turbulent and moved in like a whirlwind. His brusque, abrasive manner of speaking and of interrupting others churned people up. His was a calculated, impersonal, hurried kind of listening. Few people thought of Dudley as a person who would care about what they had to say and, consequently, tended to avoid him.

By ignoring people we may shut them off or lead them to try harder to be heard. The mother of two small children tried in vain to ignore her children on the shopping mall as they tugged at her skirt and chattered. Finally, she stopped and listened to each and then to both. Apparently they felt heard. They went dancing along at her side without further attempts to get her to listen. Parents may elicit an overdose of children's complaints because they hear them well and soothe the hurts. Parents also may catch an overdose of requests and complaints because they do not listen well. When we listen we may bring comfort, but our listening also may become a cue for others to dump their complaints. When we do not listen we may bring frustration. We may, for example, become a wall against which others throw themselves in efforts to break through.

Children may evoke characteristic responses from parents, too. Frank wonders what he does that causes his father to talk differently to him than to his two brothers. "I seem to be the one on whom he vents his frustration over them. Whenever I am home he always talks about how disorganized and how irresponsible Robert is, or how wild and uncontrollable Merrill is. My dad asks, for instance, 'Where does Merrill find those girls that he goes out with?' " Then Frank speculates, "It may be because I am much the opposite from my brothers, so dependable and so concerned about what others think of me and my friends. I have a hunch that he is wanting to be assured that he has at least one son with whom he is pleased. But I wonder if I do something to invite his criticisms of them to be assured that I get his approval."

Our patterns of listening are subject to a myriad of influences—all the ways we see one another and the ways we filter messages through our own personalities. The biases in our listening, although complicated, are not mysterious. They can be understood. The distortions can be reduced, causing clearer communication and eliciting new and freer behavior from those around us.

6. Your Appointments to Listen

Teach me half the gladness
    That thy brain must know,
Such harmonious madness
    From my lips would flow
The world should listen then—as I am listening
        now!

Percy Bysshe Shelley

Participants in seminars on psychotherapy and workshops on interpersonal relations which I conduct often engage in brief experiences to explore their barriers and biases in listening. As I introduce a series of these experiences here, you are invited to put yourself into them as completely as you can, as though you were a workshop participant.

Imagine that in fifteen minutes you have an appointment with someone who needs to talk with you. Picture yourself sitting in an office, your living room, or some other appropriate place for this appointment. The person who is coming wants to see you, but your feelings are quite different. He or she is someone you prefer not to see or hear right now. As a matter of fact, this person is one of the last people on earth you want to see. It may be someone you know, or a stranger who represents qualities that make listening and understanding difficult for you. You are waiting for the person to enter the room. Can you picture the person who is coming? Sense as fully as you can the feelings you are having about the person and about your listening for the next hour. Closing your eyes for a few seconds may help you to get in touch with your reactions. (Pause.)

The person has just entered and sat down. How would you describe your visitor? How old? What sex? What salient features in appearance or manner stand out? What is he or she coming to talk to you about? What makes this person someone you do not want to see or to hear? Are there other comments that you can make about what this person is like, why this is someone difficult to hear? (Pause.)

Imagine the interview ending now. Before considering this appointment further, I would like to ask you to picture another scene.

You have another appointment in about fifteen minutes. This is a person you may or may not know. He or she could be a composite of several people you know. Again, this person wants to see you to discuss a problem. Your appointment this time, however, is with someone you are pleased, even eager, to see and to hear. Take a few moments and think about what this person is like. (Pause.)

Your visitor has just entered the room. What might your description be? How old? What sex? What are his or her attitudes and behavior like? What concern is this person coming to share? What makes him or her someone you want to see and to hear? Any other reactions about this person, your feelings, or the appointment? (Pause.)

If you were able to imagine yourself having these appointments—one with a person you did not want to hear and the other with someone you were pleased to hear—how might you compare and contrast the two people? It is not unusual for participants in these appointment experiences to discover that distinct patterns emerge when they examine the two. Persons chosen for the unwanted appointments often are like those with whom we have had unfortunate, unhappy, and frustrating experiences. They may be people who, in our judgment, we cannot help, or those who do not like or appreciate us. Sometimes for the appointment most desired we want to see people who are likable, open to relationships with us, appreciative of whatever help we might offer. We often like to listen to people who are similar to those with whom we have had successful listening experiences and relationships. Occasionally, participants in this experience choose for their most-preferred appointments people who may not need them, or people who can offer them something in return in the relationship. Some listeners may find persons difficult to hear because of age, sex, or appearance. Others may give more importance to the nature of the problem.

In considering patterns in your choices for the *most desired* and *least desired* appointment, how important were your recent experiences in listening, either successfully or unsuccessfully, to others? Did you find yourself preferring to see someone of a particular age group or sex? Do you characteristically dislike listening to some kinds of problems while preferring to listen to others? Are the problems that you find difficult or easy to hear related to some of your own past and present concerns?

I would like to suggest a third and final appointment. This time imagine that you are the person going for the appointment. You want and need someone with whom to discuss some bothersome personal concerns. What kind of person do you wish to have for your listener? Again, it may be someone you know or a stranger with qualities you seek in a listener. Pause for a few seconds to get a picture of what the person is like with whom you have your appointment in fifteen minutes. (Pause.)

How would you describe the person you chose to listen to you? Approximately how old? A man or a woman? What is he or she like in appearance? What personality characteristics? What might you want to talk to this person about? What is there about this person that led you to choose him or her? As you consider your listener, can you see any connection between how you want this person to listen to you and the way you listen to the concerns of others? Some of us seek listeners who listen much as we do or as we wish we would. Others seek listeners who differ greatly from themselves.

Does your listener have any particular professional qualifications for understanding you? Among people who participate in this you-have-an-appointment experience, those who are in training to become psychotherapists often do not mention the technical and professional qualifications they seek in their listeners. Some of them assume that their listeners have professional training. Others see it as detracting from the personal relationship they seek. People with whom I work in training seminars seem especially interested in seeking compassionate, considerate, sensitive, and warm human beings who can understand them. These certainly are qualities to be learned and nourished, whether in psychotherapy training programs or elsewhere.

The you-have-an-appointment experience illustrates a process through which we may learn more about our attitudes in listening. The experience can be used also to recognize more clearly some of our patterns of listening to different kinds of people with different kinds of problems. Before leaving this experience, I would like to raise these final questions: When you think of the person you chose to listen to you, how do you suppose that person might feel about seeing you? Would you be thought of as someone he or she wants to hear? Or would you be regarded in some other way? What would it be like to listen to you?

OPENING UP OUR LISTENING

Can you let another person express his thoughts and feelings without criticizing or judging? Maybe you can find out the next time you have a conversation with someone, or engage in a discussion with a group of people. As you listen, check out your reactions. Are you saying to yourself: "Yes, I understand or I am trying to understand your idea or how you feel." If your intent is to understand, if you want to hear, that attitude is likely to be conveyed.

As you listen, are you looking for consistency and logic, or saying to yourself in one form or another: "I agree." "I disagree." "You are right." "You are wrong." "You feel like I do." "You are different from me." If you are judgmental and listening critically, that attitude is likely to be conveyed.

At times we want and need to evaluate carefully what is being said in terms of what we think and feel. Critical listening may be essential if we are sifting through the ideas and issues expressed by others, say, candidates for political office. Others may need to test their ideas in open discussion by having us listen critically. Listening critically and judgmentally to someone who wants and needs to be heard beyond the logic, however, may shut him or her down or lead to a defensive conversation.

If you want to experience anew your reactions to being listened to with judgmental and nonjudgmental attitudes, reverse the experience I just suggested. Search out people who listen to you in different ways. Find someone whose facial expressions, words, and gestures reflect critical judgment, perhaps skepticism toward what you are saying. Notice how you feel about talking and sharing with that person. Then find someone else who listens without signs of judging and whose expressions reflect a desire to understand, even value you, but who does not necessarily agree with what you say. Pay attention to your feelings about sharing with that person. With which listener do you feel more open, expressive, comfortable, and understood?

Listening is the other side of talking. Without listeners, there is no one with whom to talk, no one to hear us. Poor listening greatly influences how and to whom we talk. Psychological experiments suggest that listeners who show signs of hearing and accepting what is said encourage and get the speaker's attention. Those who ignore the speaker or seem to reject what is said are discouraging and are likely to be ignored in return.

I became sensitive to my own reactions the other day when I observed that, of the twelve members of a graduate seminar I am giving, four sat with expressionless faces. I noticed also that I was paying very little attention to them. My focus was on the eight students who were listening actively, talking to one another and to me. To try to change the situation, I invited the students who appeared to be nonlisteners to express their ideas and experiences related to our discussion. I assumed that a reverse cycle might be more likely to occur if they were able to talk and were heard. The result was that two began to participate—to talk and to listen actively—and two, who were especially shy, gave noticeable signs of listening, but spoke little.

Becoming actively involved with one another and with mutually interesting ideas usually opens up our listening. Admittedly, listening is only one manifestation of our attitudes. At times, we may want to explore more deeply the feelings beneath the expressionless faces and other signals that listening has stopped.

PREDICTING, ANTICIPATING

We may be able to hear one another better if we do not dwell on one another's motives for being the way we are. For me to speculate about your motives suggests that I am predicting what you are like. It also suggests that I am not open to you as the best potential source of information about yourself. When we assume that our predictions are true, we may fail to listen with precision to one another. We have already decided what we will hear—or want to hear. In the long run, knowing only my predictions about you is not helpful, since the only way I can know more completely what you think and feel is for you to tell me. Still, I may benefit from making inferences, so long as I check them out. I may infer that you are angry and inquire whether or not you are. I may infer that something joyful has happened to you and inquire whether or not you will share it. We continuously make inferences about one another from all the ways we listen to words and to behavior without words.

My anticipation of what you are about to say is different from making a prediction or assuming that I know.

In anticipating I am not leaping quite so far ahead and am more tentative than when predicting. Anticipating may keep me alert and sharpen my ability to follow a thread of thought, especially in a well-ordered statement or presentation. But the opposite may occur. In anticipating what you will say, I may dash on to my own conclusions, touch upon my own ideas or feelings, and lose contact with you.

It may be helpful for you to anticipate the remarks of friends and associates in conversation and note how your own listening is affected. You may notice that what you anticipate will vary according to the feelings you bring to the conversation and the topics of conversation. If you are feeling joyful, you may anticipate with optimism. If you are feeling guilty, you may anticipate being found out, being asked for an apology, or hearing other words that bring discomfort. I am more inclined to pick up dissatisfaction toward me from others when my own dissatisfaction with myself runs deep. At these times, I am well advised to listen more carefully and to anticipate less what they are likely to say—not an easy task. To turn the tables, in your conversation with others, do you prefer that they try to anticipate what you are about to say? Or is it better for you when the person waits and listens as you speak?

IS IT REALLY A QUESTION?

I often find myself answering questions that have not been asked. When a questioner inquires, "What do you think of the unisex trend?" does he really want to know what I think about boys and girls and adults of both sexes wearing hair the same length and dressing similarly? Perhaps the question is an opener for the one who raises it to express his own ideas and opinions on the subject. I may want to find out before launching into an answer.

"Don't you think that parents are too permissive these days?" The "don't-you-think" inquiries are seldom questions. They usually are statements that invite agreement. A few years ago I listened back to a series of tape-recorded counseling interviews and found that more than 80 percent of the comments that ended with a question mark were really statements.

The young man asks, as though talking to himself, "Why, oh why, does my father never seem to understand that I want him to listen to what I have to say, and not criticize me so much?" If you answer literally you might simply say, "I don't know." That would be true. As a person who listens literally to the words, you may be tempted to get bogged down in speculating about the father's failure to understand his son. The father is not there, of course. Speculation about his behavior is not likely to help very much. The statement we hear expresses the son's feelings and may or may not be a statement about the father's behavior. Our best bet is to hear the son who is present, rather than to speculate about the father who is not. If, as a listener, you hear the tones and see the facial grimaces, you might respond understandingly beyond the words with something like: "You just can't seem to get through to him." Or, "There seems no way to get yourself understood instead of criticized." Or, "So much criticism and so little understanding is awfully hard to take." If we want to open the conversation up by listening and responding beyond the words, we can recognize and acknowledge the feelings that were expressed in the statement couched in question form.

We use veiled questions in a variety of ways. By listening to how others use them, we can sort out more clearly how we use them. We may use such questions to open up a topic or to sound out one another on a delicate issue. We may want to test the climate of opinion or to be prepared for a face-saving retreat. If the climate is safe, we then may pose another thinly disguised question that is a statement, or we may make a statement outright. When the climate of safety is established in our relationship, our tentative questions to one another tend to diminish and our exchanges become more straightforward. We then have less need to code our messages and to decipher others' meanings.

CONGENIAL LISTENING

At the beginning of this chapter, you were invited to explore your listening attitudes by picturing—perhaps remembering—appointment experiences. In some of your scenes, listening may have been difficult, and in others easy and pleasant. Can you remember times, places, and people with whom listening seemed effortless for you? Listening in some situations may be fairly simple because of our training and experience in hearing and understanding the particular ideas or emotions expressed. Listening may be easy for us because what someone is saying "fits us" in many ways. What I hear, for instance, may fit my prejudices, ideas, and beliefs about politics, philosophy, or psychology. What I hear may appeal, like poetry, to my aesthetic senses. Listening may be soothing as it lulls me into a meditative, relaxed state. It may be energizing as it stirs up ideas or fires my imagination.

Just as some people make listening gratifying for me, I may make listening gratifying for them. Our relationship is a two-way street to enjoyable listening. They bring out my humor. I bring out their laughter. They make me feel creative and witty. I make them feel joyful. Our listening and sharing may focus on any topic—people we know, sports, automobiles. We may share bits of information hardly worth knowing, except for how we use it as a pleasurable way of being with one another.

Fortunately, not all listening and sharing has to be highly significant and focus on important problems. A good case can be made for relaxed, offhanded, and simple conversation that is free from the search for solutions, deep relationships, personal growth, or ways to change our lives. I recall with satisfaction the reminder from Joseph Wood Krutch that there is significance also in the commonplace and that a miracle which occurs every day ceases to be a miracle at all. He goes on to speak more specifically of the tiresomeness as well as the impossibility of continuous awareness of things of importance in nature and in man. He emphasizes the sensitivity with which we might see more clearly mundane daily occurrences in contrast with wonders more stimulating than our senses can absorb. "To put it more familiarly," he writes, "what I am after is less to meet God face to face than really to take in a beetle, a frog, or a mountain when I meet one."[1]

---

[1] *Baja California and the Geography of Hope,* ed. Kenneth Brower; photographs by Eliot Porter, text by Joseph Wood Krutch (San Francisco: Sierra Club, 1967), p. 22.

7. Listening Is a Way of Being

"And here is my secret, a very simple secret: It is only with the heart that one can see rightly; what is essential is invisible to the eye."

Antoine de Saint-Exupéry

In earlier chapters we have looked at how we listen to compliments and criticism, listening as a source of influence, and our barriers and biases which keep us from hearing. What has been said illustrates in varied ways that what we hear stems from our beliefs and feelings about ourselves and others as much as from what they actually say.

You and I meet on the street. With exuberance reflected in your face and voice, you exclaim, "It's really cold today." With my hands stuffed into my coat pockets and my neck pulled down into my shoulders, I soberly reply, "Yes, it is." We are not exchanging a fact about the weather so much as we are expressing our feelings about it. You like it; I do not. Each of us has heard and understood the other and the meaning of the projections of the other. If we pass at a distance and wave without another exchange, you might assume that I enjoy the cold weather as you do and I might assume that you dislike it as I do. In such an instance we would be projecting ourselves, our attitudes about cold weather, onto one another. Listening to you is always a partial projection of me since I bring myself—my feelings, expectations, and beliefs—to what you say.

By checking with each other to discover the differences and similarities between what is expressed and what is heard, we can discover better ways to share what we mean and to listen to one another. I discover, for example, that the things I think I know best may lead me to the most projection and, consequently, to the greatest distortions of what others have to say on the subject. In the extreme, I thrust myself so completely onto another person that my beliefs and feelings supersede anything that he may say. I have shut off listening to someone else and am now listening only to myself.

But if I have no projections of myself whatsoever, I bring nothing human and dynamic to our relationship. If I have experienced little and am out of touch with my own feelings, I am likely to be naive and unable to grasp the depths, the thrusts, and the power of what you feel and express.

Just as I let myself go out to another person as I listen, I also let that person come into me. Just as I project myself to some degree, I also take in the experiences of another person in the process of listening and understanding. Have you ever noticed two people in conversation, one talking with such animation and the other listening so intently that the expressions of the listener's face and the movement of his lips match those of the speaker? The identification is marked as the listener takes on many of the feelings and imitates nonverbally the behavior of the speaker. Before we do pantomimes and imitations of the behavior of others, we absorb salient characteristics that represent them. The game of charades is a kind of taking in and then letting out, a nonverbal projection of people, ideas, and incidents. Listening and understanding at both superficial and deep levels involve letting others in and letting ourselves reach out, moment to moment.

The extent to which I reach out to you and let you in while listening will depend, in part, on my willingness and ability to risk allowing my view of me, of you, and of the world to change. Some of my own beliefs, expectations, and feelings may need to be suspended temporarily if I am to listen in depth. Suspension of parts of myself and openness to you may lead me to question the core of my behavior and beliefs on occasion and may make me uneasy and vulnerable to new ideas and to my own unknown feelings. Listening deeply to hear you may at times turn out to be hazardous. But it is in such depths of listening that we meet as real people and find that stretching ourselves to get there is self-restoring.

AROUND THE EDGES

Listening for logic, for the meaning words convey, and with specific goals are ways we tease out and clarify problems and derive solutions. We listen with focused attention to ferret out complicated meanings. We listen to discover new thought relationships as ideas are put back together in different configurations. Listening with a specific focus on some occasions, however, can get in the way of hearing more comprehensive, global meanings—of hearing the "person" within and his hidden needs.

When we select only one idea or feeling for focused attention we risk getting locked into it and missing what surrounds it. If we listen and seek to define another person's problem too sharply, we may impose definitions that keep us from listening to the edges of what is being expressed. We may want to listen in some circumstances with less directed focus, with uncommitted attention, a meandering attention of sorts, to hear the words and the nuances of meaning in the quality of the voice. We watch for the signals that add meaning through gestures and body movements. We listen to the minute impressions in the context of what is expressed, what preceded it, and follows. Listening to the context, we can hear in a cumulative fashion. An experience with Martha, a college freshman, illustrates listening to broad meanings as they accumulate, as well as to specific concerns.

Martha was talking about three term papers due, time-consuming demands made by her sorority, pressure from her boyfriend to spend more time with him, and the unpredictability of her professors. There was little doubt that she was worried and frustrated. But if I can listen to her in the context of what she said a few minutes earlier, I will hear other meanings. "I always made A's in high school," she had said, "and during the fall semester here I had no trouble making good grades. But this spring semester is different. I sleep late. I miss classes. Everyone on my dorm floor wants to talk to me about her problems. And I think I have to listen. I am always tired." The messages now are more mixed.

Martha is expressing fear along with frustration. She is in conflict between meeting the demands of classes, friends, and herself as an "A" student and doing what she wants to do. But she is not clear about what she wants to do. She is having a small rebellion against herself—her good-girl-who-does-what-is-expected role versus her new I-want-to-change-something-but-don't-know-what impulse. She is now frightened and angry, and begins to feel depressed.

I speculate for a moment before listening again. Maybe, just maybe, she has not been willing to admit how frightened and angry she feels. If she has been pushing these feelings back, they can lead to depression. The depression can draw off her energy, immobilize her. There is a hopeless cyclical quality about it. More depression, less accomplishment, increased chances of failure, greater disappointment with herself, more worry, and mounting pressure to survive the semester. So the cycle goes. My sharing this likely pattern with her probably will not help her. But seeing such a pattern helps me to listen. And tuning into the depth of Martha's feelings and helping her to touch and to express them may help her greatly.

Later, as Martha could acknowledge more fully the presence of her fear and anger, and as she could express these crippling feelings, she felt less burdened. She discovered that what was happening to her was knowable, not so mysterious. With a reduction of the fear and anger, feelings of hope for surviving the semester crept in. The cycle began to reverse itself. The depression became milder and eventually lifted. In listening to Martha at first I had heard what seemed to be primarily frustrations from academic pressures. Fortunately, she was able to touch and express broader and deeper feelings as she was heard more fully. As a result, she could be helped to turn a pattern of pushed-back fright, anger, and then

105

depression into feelings of hopefulness and a desire to tackle her problems head-on.

A later interview with Martha illustrates further what may be heard in listening beyond the literal meaning of the words. I now saw the larger context of what was being expressed earlier. "I have caught up on my French and history and all the sorority chores," she announced. "But I am still behind and will be facing examinations in ten days." Her comments sounded factual, not much frustration shown, as she continued to list work she faced. Then she shifted the subject to her boyfriend. "I told him to bug off. I'll phone him when I want to talk to him again." Her anger was mounting. "He has been tooling me around, acting like he wanted to spend more time with me. He has been dating someone else. Now he says he's sorry. I'm not going to let him make up so easily."

Martha had also become assertive in other ways since I last saw her. "Don't tell me any of your problems this week," she had told her roommate. Go AWAY, the sign on her dorm door read. It had been posted for three days. She was tired of so many intrusions. Now, in a somewhat self-conscious tone, she observed, "Isn't it awful the way I have been acting?" The touch of a smile and feigned disapproval in her eyes said something else. "Sounds like you are pleased with yourself," was my reply. "Yes," she answered, grinning. "It really is awful—but nice. People I know on campus look at me as though I have changed into a mad woman." Again, Martha's pleased feelings were clear. Along with her tongue-in-cheek self-disapproval, you could hear her announcement that she was regaining control over her life and influence with people around her. The anger expressed was clear, honest, and direct. She still had much work to do, but she was not burning up so much energy stewing about it. As you listened, you could hear that her feelings were now turning more outward and less inward.

Listening loosely, letting the meaning float around, in, and through us often may bring more understanding than listening tightly, following narrow meanings of words and tight logic. Both may be important at different times. But listening whole, listening all around, listening to the edges, these are the terms that speak of the ways of listening that I have in mind now. The edges of another person's concerns—those expressions that precede and follow what is said as central in his thoughts and words—may tell us, if we listen, what he is feeling. Those edges also may tell us where his turmoil is connected, what his emotional tones are like, what is bottling up or siphoning off his energy, or what is blinding him to alternative courses of action that lie ahead.

LISTENING FOR THE THEMES

If we do not become too absorbed in listening only to the more obvious statements or to accounts of specific events, we may be able to take special notice of the wishes, worries, joys, and sadness revealed as central themes in conversations. If a friend phones you to chat for a few minutes you can listen for the themes, not as a game or to analyze, but to understand as fully as possible. The words and topics may be straightforward, but, taken with the tone qualities of the voice and the manner of sharing, they may mean more. Pervasive themes could be: I am happy and want to let you know it. I'm lonely and need you close at hand. I've been missing you lately.

107

I'm here in case you need me. I don't like the way we left each other the last time we talked. Or, simply, I like you.

Facial expressions and body posture, as well as deeds, may represent themes. Themes representing feelings of closeness or of distance may be inferred from observing body postures and positions of couples, groups of people, and families as we see them together. In therapeutic groups and in individual therapy, the nonverbal cues and the words combine to offer richer meaning to the more obvious themes of the group and to the themes of each individual.

One Man's Themes

Leo, a forty-five-year-old business executive, spent a good part of the therapy hour complaining about the cluttered appearance of his office. He was worried that important papers requiring action might be hidden in the disorganized stacks on his desk. In the same context he confided in harried tones that he was keeping piles of important papers, personal and business, in his bedroom at home. Common themes in references both to his office and to his home were, "These places are cluttered and worrisome," and at the same time, "There are important things to be done with materials there." Another underlying theme was, "And the fact that I am not doing them, not meeting my obligations, makes me feel very guilty." A corollary was, "I am a person who takes his obligations seriously—or thinks he should—but who has quit doing anything about them."

There were other themes related to Leo's secretary at the office and to his wife at home. He was pleased that his secretary had a knack for organizing his desk without misplacing important materials. She constantly pressed him to let her do it, but he agreed only occasionally. He was displeased that his wife never complained about his cluttering up the bedroom. She "lets me get by with it." Leo's themes of conflict, including his resentment toward being pushed by his secretary and wanting to be pushed by his wife, represented a greater conflict Leo was experiencing. He was struggling to decide whether or not to quit his work and change his lifestyle, to seek satisfaction in more personal ways, including travel. Moreover, in grappling with the decision, he was showing earlier behavior patterns in his desire to have a decision made for him ("my wife could give more help") and in his small rebellion against wanting and needing help ("my secretary is efficient but she is not going to run my office").

As Leo listened to the playback of the themes by the therapist, he could understand more clearly the dynamics of his dilemma. Hearing his own themes was like having a map showing where he had been and indicating clearer possibilities and prospects for where he might want to go next. The discovery that our jumbled-up feelings and conflicts can be heard and understood, and that they sometimes do make sense, is comforting and encouraging. We may then feel free to plow on into our confusion when we realize we don't have to know what it means before we express it.

Themes in Groups

Groups of people in organizations may, through their discussions, express attitudes, ideas, and concerns that add up to common themes. Several months ago, at the request of the president of an urban community college,

I spent two days meeting with seventy members of the faculty and staff. My task was, in the president's words, "to take the pulse of the campus" by getting impressions of attitudes, concerns, and hopes for the future held by faculty, staff, and administrators. In meetings with small groups, ranging in size from ten to fourteen people, I mentioned my purposes and invited reactions. Since I had worked during previous consultation activities at the college with about half the faculty and administrators present in these meetings, the discussions were lively, and problems and desired changes were freely disclosed.

By the afternoon of the second day on campus, I became aware of the recurring themes represented in the incidents, anecdotes, and concerns expressed. The first and most pervasive theme was a sense of *loss*. This theme was inferred from frequent references to faculty members who transferred to newer suburban colleges, feelings of distance between new and old faculty members, changes in composition of the student body, and complaints about lack of identification among staff members with the college as a community. With new urban campuses springing up, this oldest college was now only one of four. As a consequence, faculty and administrative staff members experienced a loss of status and of the college's attractiveness within the larger metropolitan area.

The second theme was one of *distrust*. It pervaded discussions of old and new faculty members and of growing cleavages between faculty and administration. Faculty members felt that administrators were encroaching on faculty freedoms in such matters as grading and teaching procedures. Administrators contended that too many faculty members had lost interest in student welfare and good teaching.

The third theme, characterized by feelings of being "in limbo," was *uncertainty* and *apprehensiveness*. It was represented by discussions of such questions as: Who will stay and who will go if more new campuses open? Who will stay and who will move to the new building? What happens to us if discussions of reorganization lead to changes? And, is this a place worth our continued investment?

A fourth theme, quite different, was one of *hope* and *renewal*. It was expressed in discussions of curriculum and organizational changes, of plans for new programs in new building space, and most of all, in desires among faculty members to have contacts and renewed relationships with the college president. The president was seen as a person who could lead them through these bad times as a result of his recognized leadership skills, his commitment to the college and faculty, and his considerable warmth in interpersonal relationships.

These themes and the details from which they emerged were discussed with the president, his administrative staff, and faculty representatives. They heard them clearly and tied in additional incidents, attitudes, and concerns—their own and those of colleagues—to give the themes fuller and richer meaning.

PATTERNS IN THEMES

The recurring themes expressed by an individual and by groups of individuals may, when heard and understood in a cumulative way, add up to characteristic patterns of emotional expression. I mentioned earlier that how we listen and respond to others often is biased in characteristic ways. If we gain sufficient freedom from our biased listening, we also may be able to hear how others express themselves in thematic and then patterned ways. Listening to the themes of individuals and groups of people, we may hear larger meanings and characteristic patterns in how others express love, hate, trust, wariness, and the many mixed and disparate feelings in the richness of their language.

Each of us may have numerous individual and recurring patterns for expressing dominant ways we think and feel. Minor themes of sarcasm, sharp wit, and saccharine and ingratiating deeds mixed with aggressive and withdrawing behavior, for example, might add up to a pattern for expressing anger, sometimes disguised, sometimes not. You may know people who are deeply loving and express it in oblique, diverse, but understandable ways, sometimes with attempts to disguise and sometimes not. Others we know may seem utterly lacking in guile and even may reveal innocence in their attempts at subtle deceit.

We may be fooled, of course, or unable to listen or to understand the dominant patterns of expressions in the themes of some persons. Themes that are disparate, for example, may be more difficult to hear. We may have some friends who sound almost joyful as they share bad news, and others whose announcements of good news seem enshrouded with gloom. The words and the music do not match. My grandmother used to come home crying from funerals. But when she began to talk about the people seen and the events witnessed, she sounded as though she were talking about a country festival. She showed pleasure, even joyfulness, and as a child I had trouble listening to her crying mixed with laughter. Later, when I understood that funerals were an important part of her social life, like going to church and family reunions, I could understand the pattern and larger context of her seemingly incongruous behavior.

Listening beyond the words to the themes of others is easier than listening to our own. We may develop a sensitive ear to friends and pick up their delicate signals—a plea for help, a voice of fear, feelings of hurt, jealousy, or deep appreciation. Similarly, our friends may be able to pick up the themes of our guarded messages. Unfortunately, for whatever reasons, we listen too infrequently to each other in such sensitive ways, even when we know how. It is equally possible that we listen too infrequently with heightened awareness to our own themes from day to day, those in our sounds, and those in the inner dialogues of our silence.

LISTENING AS COMMUNION

In listening we may be able to see one another as persons who seek to extend ourselves, to come out, to be what we are, and then seek to become more. Listening becomes a way through which we discover ourselves in relationships. There is a sense of movement and harmony as we feel the flow between us, back and forth, from one to the other, and then back again. To be in communication with one another in near total terms is to experience communion, a unity in which our inner and outer experiences are attuned.

Marla shares an experience from her therapy group that describes the encompassing communion-quality of listening. "Remember during the first long session when Jack talked about breaking up his marriage? He was reluctant to say much because he was absolutely convinced that no one would care, or even hear him. I had been

113

concerned for Jack, and when he began to talk I felt alone in the room with him, as if everyone else had faded away. We were, in fact, seated side by side in the group. I seemed to absorb his words and began to feel depressed, guilty, and unspeakably miserable. My internal controls were working overtime because I was crying inside and wanted to take Jack in my arms and comfort *us,* but I withheld much of my emotion, and I never touched him. I became frightened and deliberately tried to turn Jack off, but I couldn't. After he became quiet, I suddenly felt exhausted. I had cared and had heard him through my body."

Marla was intimately attuned to Jack. But only when she shared the emotions she felt could he and other members of her group know the intensity with which she had heard. And he could know that she had accompanied him on a painful journey in a wordless, almost visceral, communion.

Listening is a way of being, but also a way of doing.

8. When Someone Hears

Go to your bosom; knock there and ask
your heart what it doth know . . .

William Shakespeare

Feeling heard not only brings us into closer communion in our interpersonal journeys, it helps us to realize the depths and meaning of our own inner dialogue, even when we fear that our dialogues have stopped. When I lose for a moment my appreciation for being heard, I can sometimes recapture it by recalling incidents in my life when I was not heard.

FEELING UNHEARD

Feeling unheard may bring alienation, anger, frustration, and loneliness. It also may shut off any desire to hear others.

Peter was bogged down in a dilemma he had expressed over and over during the course of the group sessions. He was unhappy in his marriage, but could not bring himself to see it as a failure. He wanted out, but would not risk giving up the security of his home and the comfort of his two children. He was consumed with ambition, but was barely making ends meet in his limited law practice. He would not risk joining other attorneys, changing his location, or expanding his areas of practice. He was stuck, immobilized with fear and frustration.

He had begun to sound like a broken record. While trying to listen, others felt his impotence and frustration. Peter felt unheard and shut out. He sat in silence, wanting, as he stated later, "to hear no one and hoping that no one else would ever again be heard or understood in this group."

Almost daily the feeling of being unheard may arise from one situation or another. Harris was talking with a friend. "It would not be true in the least to say that my wife does not have some kind of curiosity about what I do. As a matter of fact, lately she wants to know each and every detail of my day, who I see, what is said, everything that goes on. And I haven't one foggy idea about why she wants to know. She doesn't give a damn about how I'm feeling when the day is over. When I tell her what goes on, she's not even hearing me. She's taking some kind of crazy trip of her own." Harris paused, and in a determined, vindictive tone, added, "Tonight I won't tell her!"

Being heard partially, or having your words taken over, may be as frustrating as not being heard at all. Last week Wayne, a college senior, was talking with another student and suddenly felt a compelling urge to get away from him as quickly as possible. Later he realized why. "I discovered that I had become a set of cue cards for a monologue he began to give. He would hear just enough of what I said to latch onto my subject and then take off with it and make it his. He never seemed to care about whether I finished a sentence, or even whether I heard him. He just talked on and on, filling in with words."

Being unheard may not always be bad. "My roommate and I do not always listen to each other when we talk about our problems and daily events," Elaine said. "But we know that each cares about the other. During the times that we both need to talk, I say something about one thing and her comment is in a totally different ball park. I come back with topic number one again and she responds with something else about her own topic. And so it goes—my topic, then hers, or new topics for each. We laugh at ourselves when we realize that we are both going on and on in our own little worlds. An hour, a day, or a week later one of us may come back to the crazy exchange, and we find out that we're not so confused as we thought. We even remember things that we didn't think we heard."

When we feel cut off and alone, we may try to make contact with others by our attempts to hear and to understand them. Marcella, an attractive professional woman in her early thirties, was regarded as a catalyst for members of a weekend marathon therapy group. When others spoke she leaned forward, looked at them intently, and responded in words that reflected understanding. It was soon clear that Marcella could hear and could let others know it. As the weekend wore on, however, people paid less and less attention to Marcella; they seemed to withdraw from her. As a consequence, she withdrew. When she could no longer fend off her own feelings of isolation, she let them out in tears and deep sobs of despair. Marcella had deluded herself into believing that her hearing of others was a gift to them when actually it was a shield against involvement with them and herself—an attitude they soon sensed. What she needed was to be heard and to feel that someone could be with her in her loneliness.

A HUMAN CONNECTION

Friendships are sometimes begun from hearing another person and discovering an affinity of feelings. Occasionally the identification with the other person is so complete that one knows what is to be said beforehand. The feeling is eerie—something of a déjà vu experience, as if the conversation had happened exactly like this before. Jeanne and Joyce began a strong friendship which lasted for years from an experience in which they felt that each was speaking for the other. "It was not just that Joyce was expressing similar feelings," Jeanne said. "She was saying the very words that I had said before, in just the same way that I wanted to say them now. It was kind of spooky. I had this terrific feeling of identification with her. I really understood everything she was saying. When I let her know, she could hear and understand me the same way. That was even spookier. Yet, neither of us was really surprised. Strange, isn't it! From that time on we felt a bond. We don't always understand each other that completely, but we did that night and it seemed to have cemented our friendship."

Relief may be found in the discovery that you are not alone, that someone else knows what you are feeling. A special joy may arise when someone shares experiences and feelings that you thought were uniquely yours. Henrietta and Alice were comforted by one another in their concerns over what to do about children. Neither could have children. Both were fearful of adopting a child because of the unknowns. What might an adopted child's birth parents be like? Would it be possible to love an adopted child as one's own? Would there be heartbreaking surprises in how a child might turn out? Still, they wanted to "risk it" if they could get the courage. Others in the group were asked if they felt involved in some way with the concerns Henrietta and Alice were facing.

"I do," Phil said softly. He had not spoken much in the group. Slightly embarrassed, he looked first at Alice and then at Henrietta. "I'm twenty-one now, and I have wondered for years if my parents had regrets about me." He paused and then added, hesitantly, "They adopted me."

Alice and Henrietta could not hide their embarrassment. Before Alice could get beyond, "I'm sorry, I never thought about—" Phil cut in to ask her not to feel badly and to reassure her that she had not upset him. "You simply reminded me of some things I've never really forgotten."

Dora quickly intervened. "Alice, maybe you and Henrietta would like to know more about what it's like from the other side, in case you do decide to adopt children."

Before they could answer, Phil shot a glance at Dora, as though he had just recognized an old friend. "You too?" he asked.

"Yes, me too," she replied.

Within a couple of minutes Phil and Dora were sitting in the center of the room with Henrietta and Alice, telling them about their good and bad times as adopted children. They told also about some of the things they had imagined about their known and unknown parents. They shared incidents about how they fared with children who had not been adopted.

It was unmistakably clear that Dora and Phil felt less alone in the group with the knowledge of one another's adoption. They had begun to feel a unique camaraderie

121

in sharing and comparing experiences. Alice and Henrietta, who found solace earlier in the fact that they viewed their problems similarly, were now getting an entirely new perspective. To those of us on the edge of their animated exchanges, it was undeniable that the four of them were feeling a very special human kinship. They were reaching out and touching one another, and they were feeling the exhilaration of it.

BEING HEARD:
PRELUDE TO HEARING OTHERS

Almost always we listen to ourselves as we listen to others. We seldom by-pass ourselves. The echoes of our thoughts and feelings reverberate within us and influence what we hear and how we respond. To know what we are saying to ourselves is a prelude to listening and hearing someone else. But sometimes we cannot listen clearly—either to ourselves or to someone else—until we are heard by someone who can play back what we are saying and help us to find out what is going on inside. When we are heard we hear better. A chain reaction of sorts may be set in motion.

Years ago a college senior in one of my classes came for a conference. She was working part time as a dorm advisor to freshmen, and, after talking about the class, she stayed to talk about how weighted down she felt listening to so many girls with seemingly insoluble problems. For an hour she described their problems and her worries about them. The next day she stopped by to announce that she had discovered something quite wonderful. "When you listened to me without taking over my worries," she said. "I found out that I could listen better to them." Then she asked, "I wonder if I might come by once in a while to let off a little steam when hearing their problems gets me down?" As she was walking out she looked back over her shoulder and then stopped. I was struck by her appreciation for what it is like to be heard, when she asked, "But is there someone who will then listen to you?"

Being heard, then listening to another person, and discovering that the other person can now listen back—the chain reaction that I mentioned—are illustrated in an experience with Martin, a fifteen-year-old boy struggling to become more independent from his highly critical father. He spent early therapy sessions between tears and anger over his frustration and conflict. He cared very much about his father but at times also hated him. He wanted to talk and to have his father hear, but he saw the prospect as hopeless. Each try seemed to end with Martin or his father becoming overly critical and withdrawing in anger. Their relationship was at stalemate. In Martin's view, his father discredited his ideas and kept him feeling unsure, dependent, and fearful of trying to work out a better relationship.

During those early sessions we engaged in role-playing situations involving father-son transactions in which Martin would be the son and I the father; then we would switch the roles. In the role-playing episodes, Martin was surprised to discover how much he whined and behaved in childish ways. As a consequence he became eager to try different ways to express himself more clearly, and he practiced listening to his father. These learning experiences helped Martin understand his relationship with his father but were insufficient to change the relationship drastically. Martin fell back into feelings of futility about prospects for a happier relationship with his father.

At the end of one interview, after talking about disturbing conflicts and the hopelessness of the situation, Martin decided to give up on his father for awhile. He would seek relationships with other adults and with new friends. Attempts to form new relationships, he thought, might make him feel better. Having made this decision, he appeared relieved, as though he had relinquished a heavy burden. Moreover, I was able to give up some of my own needs to improve the situation immediately and markedly.

Martin came into the next interview smiling, as though he had a happy secret. He had taken a different stance in talking with his father. "I simply went up to Dad and said, 'I'm tired of being mad at you. I'm unhappy and worried and want to change it if it's possible.' At first Dad looked skeptical, like he didn't trust me. For a minute I was scared and almost backed down. Then I decided to stay with him. He fussed at me for not coming sooner to talk to him this way. And I said, 'Well, I'm here now.'

"And then he started to listen to me. And another thing. I sat there and listened to him. Oh, he still gripes and criticizes, but I'm not as afraid or upset about that now. I don't expect it to last, but I know that I can get him to listen a little, and I can try to listen back." As Martin began to listen to himself in a safe situation, to experience being heard, and to reduce his paralyzing need to win approval, he was able to "listen a little" and to help his father listen too.

Much is said about the need for parents to listen to their children. It seems equally important that children learn to listen to their parents, not simply as people who tell them what to do, but as people who need to be heard and understood. Children who can hear and understand their parents often discover that they help their parents learn to listen back. I find that when my children have been able to hear me as a person who happens to be their father, they add to my ability to listen back and to our mutual respect and growth. In this way children can help parents to grow up too.

People in the helping professions and those with whom we work, as well as children and their parents, can help one another to hear. All may grow in the process. Those among us who happen to work in the mental health professions as "professional listeners" (I bridle at the term as I write it) may come to believe that we have special built-in powers for true listening. True, we may be sensitive and perceptive, and we may have sharp skills for listening, but they need to be honed regularly.

If we also teach and supervise others who are training for the helping professions, we may be especially vulnerable to the myths of our own infallibility. We may need help from people we supervise, as well as from colleagues, family, and friends, to tease out our listening distortions, so that we do not take for granted that what we hear is "objective hearing."

PERSONAL VULNERABILITY

Despite receiving help to reduce my own distortions in hearing, I often have trouble listening openly and allowing others to be free and separate from me. Such hearing difficulties recur even though my experiences tell me that, when I hear and relate to others in ways that encourage their separateness and freedom, they usually make decisions appropriate for them. There are exceptions, of course; some individuals and groups of people, given freedom, continue to behave in self-defeating ways.

Carl Rogers, talking about a therapeutic relationship, speaks to the issue when he writes: "To me it appears

125

that only as the therapist is completely willing that *any* outcome, *any* direction, may be chosen—only then does he realize the vital strength of the capacity and potentiality of the individual for constructive action. It is as he is willing for death to be the choice, that life is chosen; for neuroticism to be the choice, that a healthy normality is chosen." [1] In and out of therapeutic relationships I experience the faith of which Rogers speaks. Yet, my faith falters sometimes when I care in deeply personal terms about the other person. It falters when for some reason I become too enmeshed in the conflicts, struggles, or aspirations of people confronting their personal problems.

Rogers has referred many times in his writing and speaking to nonpossessive love and a deep caring that allows others to be free, with no controlling strings attached. I have experienced that kind of love. I have experienced its opposite too—love and caring that are too possessive. It is this latter kind of caring and its attendant conflicts that I am talking about here, relationships in which I become a part of the problem and confound the options, attitudes, and behavior of others with my own. My emotional involvement makes me personally vulnerable. As a consequence I may be less willing for others to be completely separate and free from me. In the extreme I may become fearful, controlling, and unable—unwilling too—to entrust them with personal freedom of choice. In such a predicament I may come to believe that their choices and behavior become statements about me and my behavior.

The other persons and I may begin to find relief and ways out of the restricted relationship if I can talk openly

---

[1] Carl R. Rogers, *Client-Centered Therapy* (New York: Houghton Mifflin, 1951), pp. 48–49.

and directly about my own concerns in the relationship. It may be necessary for me to talk about my fears and my need to control to protect myself from hurt. If others can hear and understand me—as painful, embarrassing, and frightening as the process may be—the results can be gratifying. I may discover anew that what I have been able to offer someone else at other times but am unable to offer now—the desire and ability to listen openly and freely, as a separate but caring person—has now been offered to me. Others thus help me to begin to experience once again a measure of my own separateness and freedom. And in the process they may gain in their own ability to listen and in their sense of renewal.

Times remain, however, when I do not confront my feelings of personal vulnerability in relationships with others, and my listening and the relationships remain impaired. And when I am closed off from others, I am less able to hear myself or them freely and fully.

WHEN SOMEONE TRULY HEARS

The capacity to hear ourselves is a key to sensitive understanding of our human desires and needs. "A man is never so serene," writes Wendell Johnson, "as when he hears himself out, granting to himself the quieting freedom to speak fully without fear of self-reproach. Nor is he ever so gravely ill as when he stops his tongue with crying out 'Shame! Shame!' unto himself. . . . By stopping up our own ears against the sounds of our own voices we achieve not the peace of inner stillness, but the unnerving disquietude of haunted consciousness." [2] Our minds may

---

[2] Wendell Johnson, *Your Most Enchanted Listener* (New York: Harper, 1956), p. 21.

stop the sounds of our own inner voice, and hearing ourselves may become impossible when our thoughts and feelings are puzzling, conflicting, or distressing. We may regain the ability to hear again when someone else has heard us and helped us to know and to express what is there.

Demanding clarity about thoughts and feelings before sharing them can be a real problem. It is for me, and I cannot always meet the demand. What I need is to share my jumbled-up inner dialogue with someone who can hear, and, in listening, can help me to hear myself. With help, I may find release from the captivity of my own words and touch delicate, frightening, or other eclipsed feelings within me.

I am more likely to risk letting out my thoughts and feelings if someone is not judging me right or wrong, consistent or inconsistent; not diagnosing and attaching labels; not pressing for logic or clarity. I do more than enough judging, labeling, and pressing for answers as I listen to myself. When I press too hard and doggedly for total understanding, I get bottled up, and stop up the sounds inside.

I want someone to hear my thoughts and feelings *as they are expressed* and to touch with me the different shades, textures, and patterns of what I feel. I want someone to allow the tentativeness, uncertainty, and ambiguity that may be there from moment to moment. When my inconsistencies are heard as natural and expected, like parts of a puzzle that may fit when all are found, I am more likely to find obscure and previously concealed feelings. Incongruous emotions and thoughts may blend toward a unified pattern, or they may stay loose and apparently irreconcilable. Either way I often find release, more inner harmony, and less tension with myself, largely because of the way someone can hear and free me to hear what is there.

The other day I reread some comments Carl Rogers shared on what it was like for him when he felt heard. He wrote: "A number of times in my life I have felt myself bursting with insoluble problems, or going round and round in tormented circles or, during one period, overcome by feelings of worthlessness and despair. . . . I have been able to find individuals who have been able to hear me and thus to rescue me from the chaos of my feelings . . . who have been able to hear my meanings a little more deeply than I have known them. . . . I can testify that when you are in psychological stress and someone really hears you without passing judgment on you, without trying to take responsibility for you, without trying to mold you, it feels damn good. . . . It has permitted me to bring out the frightening feelings, the guilts, the despair, the confusions. . . . It is astonishing how elements which seem insoluble become soluble when someone listens. How confusions which seemed irremediable turn into relatively clear flow-streams when one is heard." [3]

A note from a woman in her late thirties to her therapist expresses what it was like for her to have someone hear and respond from within as a person: "I vividly remember coming to see you one particularly important evening. The wind was rising; a thunderstorm was brewing. A storm was brewing inside me, too. My mouth was

---

[3] Carl R. Rogers, "Some Elements of Effective Interpersonal Communication," talk given at California Institute of Technology, Pasadena, Calif., Nov. 9, 1964, p. 4.

dry, and I was so frightened. You came and stood close beside me and said, 'Must you carry the burden all alone?' With those words you gave me permission to lean on you, literally, too. And that was the first time after all those years that I could speak of my terror and anger and feelings of utter abandonment. I had felt for so long that no one could hear me. When you said that you knew how awful it had been, I knew that you knew. And your knowing took the stings of pain and fright out of it—and I could feel quietness inside."

Sometimes I feel lonely and forlorn and experience a pervading sense of failure in my life. I wonder whether I or anything that I do has any worth. I want to give up. I feel doubts about long-held values that have served me well and offered hope. I feel little energy or inclination to reach out to seek relief from the despair, and certainly brook no thoughts or strivings toward becoming a better or more effective person.

Whenever and wherever such overwhelming feelings occur, I need very much to be heard. But, as I have been suggesting, it is at just such times that I may not risk asking to be heard. In different ways I may, instead, move away from people who might hear me best and who might care the most.

A few years ago I was in anguish. My life had become painfully burdensome for the moment. It was dusk, and I was standing on the deck at the back of my home looking toward the hills in the distance and feeling distant from all the world. My younger daughter, who was eleven at the time, sensed my unspoken despair. She stood beside me, slipped her arm around my waist, and said softly, "It's okay if you want to cry, Daddy." All the dammed-up turbulence within me, so resolutely guarded, broke loose. Still she stood beside me in both tenderness and strength.

I felt a mixture of freedom and fright, of appreciation and wonder, of embarrassment and relief. And I knew that in the guise of being strong, I did not have to hide deep anguish ever again—at least from her . . .